JOHN WAIN

POEMS

1949–1979

JOHN WAIN

Poems

1949–1979

821
WAI

© John Wain 1956, 1961, 1965,
1969, 1976, 1978, 1979, 1980

ISBN boards 0 333 28789 4
ISBN paper 0 333 31356 9

First published 1980 by
MACMILLAN LONDON LIMITED
4 Little Essex Street London WC2R 3LF
and Basingstoke
Associated Companies in Delhi, Dublin
Hong Kong, Lagos, Melbourne
New York, Singapore and Tokyo

Photoset in Great Britain by
ROWLAND PHOTOTYPESETTING LIMITED
Bury St Edmunds, Suffolk

Printed in Hong Kong

ACKNOWLEDGMENTS

Of the poems not previously collected in
book form, some have appeared in periodi-
cals, viz. *New Poetry, Oxford Poetry Now,
Poetry London Apple, The Lugano Review, The
Seneca Review, Argo, and Labrys.*

Dedication

I find myself rather austere about dedications; I do not believe, as some writers seem to, that a poem can be dedicated to one person and then taken back and given to another; nor that a book of poems can be dedicated to A and virtually every poem in the book to C, D, E and so on, till A gets only the end-papers. To me, once a poem is given to someone, it stays with them for ever, and a book of poems is a single nosegay. *A Word Carved on a Sill* was dedicated to Marianne, *Weep Before God* to Nevill Coghill, *Wildtrack* to my sons, *Letters To Five Artists* to the ghost of Django Reinhardt, and *Feng* (not represented here) to Peter Levi. That leaves just the new crop, the poems in the first part of the book, and I dedicate those to James Russell Grant, poet, physician, seer, and my friend for twenty-five years.

Contents

Author's Note

This is not my 'collected poems'; I don't believe anyone under about sixty-five should start talking in those terms; it is what is known in the trade as a 'new and selected'.

I have reprinted the poems exactly as they stand, my view of revision being that a poem dating from an earlier period was written by one's earlier self, and to rewrite it is to tamper with someone else's property. One twenty-year-old poem I have shortened slightly, because very soon after publishing it I realised that it was a good idea spoilt by being dealt with at too great length; and a lyric from *Wildtrack* ('Rich blood disturbed my thought') incorporates the minor changes I have instinctively made, these ten or a dozen years, in reading the poem to audiences. Apart from that, nothing is changed.

The earliest poem here, the last in the book, was written in 1949; I like it and would in any case have reprinted it, but I also admit to finding a pleasurable neatness in the fact that the presence of a poem from that date (it is some years earlier than anything else here) makes the selection stretch over thirty years. It does not set out to cream off everything of interest; there is, I hope, plenty of substance among the large bulk of material I have not selected, particularly in *Wildtrack* and *Letters to Five Artists*, while *Feng* (1975) is not represented here at all, because it is in print and needs to be read entire. But I hope it gives the thoughtful reader enough material to form a judgment on my work as a poet over the last three decades – a judgment that will release me from any need to look backward, and set me free for the work that is to come.

Oxford, 1979   J.W.

New Poems

1978–1979

Visiting an Old Poet

Visiting an Old Poet

As I walked from the village to his house
along that curving half-mile of road, I thought,
It's twenty-two years. And I almost turned back.

But when I came through the door, and saw him
sitting on the sofa in the long cool room
and he looked up, and smiled, and knew me, I thought:
This will be good. And at once came the next thought,
not separate, two blossoms on the one spray,
It would be fitting to make a poem for him.

I knew he was old.
Everyone knows it. His oldness has become
the chief thing they know about him: *old, old, old.*
Most of the people who run the world,
who run the publishing houses, the studios,
the news agencies, the people who pay your fare
to go and see him and write something interesting –
they were not born and their parents were not born,
when he was young and stubborn and full of sap
and running over with poetry, when he was savage
sarcastic and funny, when he cut rough capers
across respected graves with waxen lilies
under domes of glass: splintering the domes,
breaking the pale wax petals.
                              Oh Lord of life,
where were you keeping them, the not-yet-born,
back in the days of his youthful sun and rain?
Were they full of hope, little half-formed bat-souls
beating their leather wings against the glass
to get into the lighted, scented world?
Or were they torpid at the end of the cave,
hanging in clusters, unwilling to come down,
feeling secure as long as their hooked claws

held on to the rough cold roof?
　　　　　　　　　Did they ever want
the world as it is, with all its wheeling fires
and exploding stars?
　　　　　　　But he wanted it, he
ran forward, sometimes crazed with panic, sometimes
falling headlong and covering his eyes
because of the terror of the living world:
but always rising again when the fit had passed,
climbing shakily first to his knees
then, gasping, to his feet, an upright man,
a man silhouetted against terror and joy.

So I entered the house and I saw his body
sitting where it had sat two decades before,
in the same stance, or only a little slackened:
in the same clothes, or the same kind of clothes.

It was his soul, of course, that I wanted to touch –
his vibrant, feeling web of inner truth:
not prod and poke it like a farmer, nor
assess it knowingly like an auctioneer,
but gently and respectfully question it, and receive
some rays of its light, some particles of its warmth,
so long as I was not robbing him of strength,
not draining his spirit. (I need not have worried.
His strength is not less than it always was,
though in some ways it is different.) Approaching his
　　　soul
I had to walk down the avenue of his body,
or rather clamber that rock-strewn mountain pass
where one can see the marks of old violences –
the whitened bones of animals and men,
and giant trees snapped off by bounding rocks:
for this, in the thawing season, was avalanche country.

And so I touched his body, and spoke to it.

8

(Once, after a silence, he put his hand on mine.
It felt like just-dried clay. And he said 'Cold.')

So of course as we sat together I asked myself,
What is it, then, to talk with a man's body?

Is the body a shell?

Is the body a highway?

What is the body, is it a cave
where the soul goes to get messages?

Perhaps that is it, perhaps it is a cave
where the soul knows a word will be spoken,
either by the sybil who lives at the far end of the cave
or by the god of freedom who now and then
puts his handsome bearded face into the cave
softly laughing, and then speaking a word:
or not speaking at all, just dancing for a moment
in the casual likeness of a jet of water.
Or perhaps some wild animal who has crept
into the cave for shelter, in adversity,
hunted, or pinched by a hard frost,
will crouch behind a rock somewhere in the cave
and utter a cry, and the cry will come out as a word:
and the soul will hear it as a word,
and understand, and come out satisfied:
will leave the cave of the body, quietened,
satisfied and answered.

Notice that I do not ask what the soul is.
(Ah there, Walt! You invented this idiom,
this kind of talking and questioning in a poem:
and you were an old poet, too, in time,
and people visited you in Camden, New Jersey:
ah there, Walt! I have always loved you too.)
Notice, I say, that I do not ask what the soul is,
everybody knows that, it is too obvious.

The soul is not an entity but a process.
It is a state of accepting and co-ordinating:
the pattern of a dance when the limbs that were dancing
have sunk to rest, the toss of a green bough
in the wet spring wind, after the tree has fallen:
the flutter of a white handkerchief waved in farewell,
when the handkerchief is folded and put away:
the pattern, the toss, the flutter, these go on,
and these are the soul. Everyone knows that.

★

Age, in its bodily manifestations, arouses our pity,
when the sinews shorten and cramp, the muscles dissolve,
eyesight and hearing dim, movement is vague:
but age I find not pitiable in fulfilled men.
It completes the triumphal arch of their life.

For this poet, it is not his eight decades
or not they only, that make the condition of age,
but the stillness that has fallen upon his mind
as gently as snow while the brain was hushed in sleep
and the eyes were not looking.
                                When they opened again
to the light, and the brain renewed its registering,
the stillness had come, the man at last was old.
Now decisions are made only by the body's declension.
He listens only to the susurrus of time
who once heard the eagle's shriek from the farthest
        mountain,
the most distant rasp of the shy raven,
the vixen's scream in the darkest of thickets.
Where once he moved towards change as a feeder of life
now he waits for the change that moves towards him.
But the waiting has its richness too: in patience
and in fulfilment it hears its own clear music,
a music for the accepting spirit to dance to,
making sense of the movement of his feet

10

as it was then, and as it had to be,
long years ago, and yesterday, and now.
It was not senseless wandering after all.
It was a dance, across a patterned floor.
The music rounds it out: he hears, and sees.

★

His poems bloom around him, flowers
planted with the seed of his fresh hours.

He set them in the ground to bloom
when he was strong and desirous as a bridegroom.

Now his strength has left him, but theirs
is always renewed in colours and fragrant airs.

At rest amid an energy he no longer needs
he breathes calmly while all urgency recedes.

He is patient as a statue of rained-on stone.
There will be no more poems now the bird has flown,

the magic bird that came and went silently
scattering poem-seeds from the cloud-dappled sky.

But he does not grieve, he no longer needs the bird,
content to wait now for the one unknowable word

to form in the cool silence of his stilled brain:
the human songs are over, earth's loss is heaven's gain,

or the gain of whatever it is lies ahead
across the gulf of death, when the old skin is shed,
and the one unknowable word is finally said.

★

So far, my unambitious poem has crept
close to the ground: the rhythms of talk, and easy
rhymes. But enough. Rise, winged horse! Fly, Muse!
Soar nearer to your subject, give strain for strain,
paean for paean. You celebrate a singer,

11

not of shanties or cool cabaret ditties, but
a robed singer, a lofty builder, a patient carver
of masks for the great truths!

★

I think of his life. Divagations enough:
from many vessels he slaked the one deep thirst:
passion and the need for passion were his themes:
his heart's goal was the never-remaining moon,
he lived by day in the light of his night's dreams:
the same sacred madness in the last as in the first,
the immortal garment woven from mortal stuff.

Each straight-backed and fine-nostrilled youthful queen
hair of raven's wing or of cornfield
paused in her dancing when he spoke the needful word,
halted amid the shine of the travelling moon
in homage to his need as still as a stone bird
against ripple of water and a sky where stars wheeled:
as if his hunger for her was the first truth she had seen.

How shall we see this need? With pity? A common man's
    itch?
Many would deny it the crown and title
of love, which they say takes root and holds, holds
and is the only constant thing beneath the moon.
But surely passion, which unweariedly gives and unfolds
finding in each queen beauties beyond recital
is love as we know it, or something just as rich:

on hot summer days, in the woods, I have often waited
amid calm thickets where light was an emerald slant
with hope, sometimes fulfilled, to hear the nightingale
who seeks the day's green tent and the night's clear moon:
and surely I loved when, shy and hidden as a snail,
I listened with wonder to the sudden divine descant
from the small feathered throat, a bird not separated

from nightingale-nature, sharing its bird-delight
with man-delight, or rather not caring
what becomes of the notes once they have been released
into the green calm. And it is the one moon
he gives fealty to, though her form has never ceased'
to round or slim as she sails through the dark, never
    wearing
the same shape twice nor the same fullness of light.

If I, entranced listener, love one nightingale
as much as another, since the music is the same,
so he has loved women. Can I feel surprise
that he, whose map of truth is the face of the moon,
should have loved moon-nature and woman-nature in
    whatever guise
they chose to appear? His fire was one constant flame,
though fuelled by the changing female and the changing
    male.

            ★

'He has no memory.' Sequence matters less
when you are living in an endless now.
What did he have for breakfast? Which
breakfast – today's or the one that ended his childhood,
that morning when he stood, in a sharp collar,
by a family fireplace suddenly grown strange,
packed, labelled, waiting for the station cab
to go to school and eat and sleep with strangers
for ever and ever? Or the breakfast he carried
to his first bride on their first waking-up
in their own rumpled bed? (He timed the eggs
in the sunny kitchen, drunk with her shadowed hair.)
Which breakfast? The stiff rashers he chewed and gagged
    on
waiting beside the fire-step, under the sandbags
with dawn staining the sky, and bayonets fixed
and every man's face drawn to a mask of death?
Which breakfast did he eat today? He lives

13

beyond the reach of time as it reaches me.
Sequence? What is it but an arrangement of time?
And time in itself is nothing: a neutral accretion.

Time is an emptiness that acknowledges
it must be filled somehow, with some nature.

Last night I smelt the air that moved across
the meadows, after a long day's sun
on ground that had been soaked. The grass and flowers
flavoured the air, and the breath and harmless dung
of the slow-moving animals. I breathed, and my breath
        was prayer.
Yet the air was just air. And time is just time.
Sometimes I see it as a clear liquid
waiting to be tinctured by a drop of thought.

There are red thoughts, and purple thoughts, and green
        thoughts,
and thoughts of slate colour, waiting to colour time.
The transparency of time is offensive to nature:
it is more, it is a contradiction,
it is forbidden by the law of the universe.
There is no such thing as the clear liquid time.
That is what time would be if left to itself,
but it is not left to itself.
                                I say time is thought.
Without thought it is forbidden to exist.
Even the rocks and pools have consciousness.
Clay and sand think in their calm fashion.
Much more the plants, more still the animals,
most of all we who are walking dream-cages.

To think about anything is to change its nature.
A new thing, that has never been thought about
exists over-simply in its two dimensions.
It needs to impinge, and to be thought about.

Our dog sleeps on an old blanket. He twitches

and growls, then breathes softly. When the blanket was
new
it was just a folded blanket in a warehouse.
Then it was bought and carried to a bed,
where it kept people warm while they slept or talked,
or made love or quarrelled. And sometimes while they
died.
In its old age it slid from bed to floor.
We gave it to him when he was a puppy,
to reassure him when he was left alone.
He needed it then because it smelt of us:
now, it smells of him.   The blanket is time,
and time is the breath and growl of the sleeping dog,
and the people making love and keeping warm,
and quarrelling, and letting the blanket slip
from bed to floor. Time is sweat, and thought, and
kisses.

The sequence does not matter. Time is a cube.
If it happened once it is still happening.
The dog sleeps while the couple kiss and the man dies:

the creak of the mattress as the dying man
stiffens for the last time with open sightless eyes
is the same creak as when he lays her down.
And the dog groans, 'It all happens for ever.'
He lays his ears down flat and sleeps again.

★

So I encountered his body. This was not trivial.
It was still upright and convivial.

His body moved slowly. Inside it, soul stirred.
I touched the cage bars and looked in at the bird.

Facing him, I came back once more to that question:
does soul follow body's every suggestion,

15

or is body the servant, the snarling Caliban,
feeling cheated without soul, feeling less than a man,

so that soul must be renewed in him over and over?
(Yet renewal's true spring and source he can never
    discover.)

You could plot this poet's life by his body's story,
the steps by which soul climbed to its last promontory.

★

Three times his body lived. In youth, it fought:
knew death: survived: in fecund middle years
it loved and nurtured, calming children's fears
and rousing women to its strength. Such thought

sustained him till the blood past action cooled.
And then his body slept. In dreams it moved
towards the souls and bodies it had loved,
thence to the knowledge-grove where dreams are
    schooled.

Who taught our blood to seek out answering blood
coursing in rhythms that complete our own,
he asked: did body? soul? or some high mage

licensed by God to marrow lifeless bone
with energy? What master found it good
to flood us with love's rage that seeks love's rage?

★

I, poet caught in sharp cross-winds of trouble
visited a poet at rest among his harvest's stubble.
His field was reaped and the full sheaves were in the barn.
May frost and mildew never come to do them harm.
May his last days be bright and calm as this June evening
and when death comes may it glide on level wing:
and may he, who made life's grit into pearls for a necklace
teach me always that art should be considered but life
    reckless.

Horses

Horses

Heavy fringed feet
slipping and stamping on the short steep hills

iron-rimmed wheels
grinding on cobbles, creak and chink of harness

as the sweat-suppled
collar leans to the strain of a ton's drag:

a ton of hay, a ton
of coke, a ton of flint, a ton of money

to fly on crisp
green-rustling Bank of England wings or bunch

into a fat gold
cloud and thunder sovereigns down to wherever

money mucks in
to flower as country homes with gravel drives

and the young master's
household-name school with ivy and long elms:

away, beyond
that hazed horizon with slag-tips and farms.

The horses pull
nostril-dilated, snorting, and the men

with calloused hands
walk with them, say their names, bring round their
        heads

their patient heads
that understand the weight of earth and sky.

★

Why horses? because the wheels
could never afford to stop

19

turning, so the hoofs
must clop-clop ahead of the
wheels, the big fringed feet
ahead of the iron-rimmed
wheels with their heavy spokes
of timber, and the men
with ungloved hands could
never afford to stop
walking beside the big patient
heads; turning them, turning them.

O they could never afford
to stop: Master in his house
with the gravel drive, Young
Master under his elms, the shareholders,
the work-force, the Empire,
yea, all which it inherit, would go
splat and vanish if they ever
stopped, splat like a mud bubble
into surrounding blackness.
Or so they all believed. Believed, and worked.

Come with me: it's easy: dangle
in a snug basket or ride my
back, boy-on-a-dolphin style, but either
way, come, and share my aerial
surveillance of my pre-beginnings,
the Ur-history of an individual
stubborn and free-wheeling, yet always
suspecting that he moves in
cut grooves, traces a diagram
marked out in sepia-tinted
years: and marked as much
by weather and animals as by ancestors.
My Ur-history is the sweat and heartbeat
of horses, as much as anything: not
lean-bellied racers, glossy hunters or
the dappled spit-and-polish mounts of

impassive guardsmen or the wary
police, no, work-horses, bred
for muscle-power and long obedience.

★

Now we tilt north and west: the air smells fresher:
Our shadow falls across the fields of Cheshire.

Unsheltered, featureless, no painter's vistas:
a place for diggers-in and dour resisters.

Flat, wooded country. No hills. Some ridges.
Dull-gleaming canals and little humped bridges.

Dark red-brick farms and barns. Clatter of pails.
Chester a distant smudge: and further, Wales

where the flat country ends and language changes:
gnarled oaks, black cattle, little stubborn ranges

of those primeval mountains, old when Earth
was new. They have their truth, they know their
    worth.

Theirs not to toil and spin, not to produce.
Here on the plain, the earth is made for use:

the plough, the wagon, milk, and sheaves of grain.
I grew out of these fields. They call me Wain.

★

So there they are: rooted. Stayers
in one place. No layers

of perception and response, just the one
flat bench for their spirit to work on.

Or so you'd think, seeing them. But
the mind burrows madly in its deep rut:

these people have dreams, and longings, yes,
even these people. Try to guess

what glowing images could ever fuel
dreams in these limbs and brains. The cruel

load of day-labour pins them down
in the wind-badgered field or rectangular town:

if they wander a few paces from the track
of wage-work, a voice warns 'Get back,

get back for the milking, the kiln-firing,
lay down meekly your dreaming and desiring,

drop your longings like discarded tools,
let them rust by the discoloured pools

left by the cold rain in the cart-ruts.
Green jungle parrots and sweet coconuts

are not more alien to your narrow patch
than dream-eggs of pleasure which never hatch.'

And what of the needs that burn, early and late?
O palliate, says the oracle, palliate,

find a girl within a few streets,
rock her fiercely between lawful sheets:

then children: she's older, and tired
and Love is a master who once hired

both of you on a lifetime contract.
Forget that first glad shock of contact

and learn to see life as a cart-wheel
with an iron rim. Not paid to feel

and certainly not encouraged to dream,
your basic metaphor is the work-team:

the plodding alliance of man and horse
or man and wife, with some love of course

or at least some habit and good-nature
to soften Existence his grim feature:

and yet they dream, I promise you that they do,
huge coloured shapes come slowly moving through

the white landscape of each sleeping mind
like ornate balloons that drift and never find

anchorage that could be shown on a chart,
yet carrying food for the starved heart

which they let fall haphazard over the roofs
and chimneys. Nor are any reproofs

provoked or anxieties stirred:
a balloon is not menacing like a giant bird,

it floats gently above landscape and steeple:
it does not tyrannize the sleeping people

where they lie gently curled, body to body:
it practises only its gentle psalmody,

feeding their sleep with the things they hunger
    after,
some sense of joy and movement, surprise and
    laughter.

And the long foreheads of the horses, do they
    shelter
dreams of rest in a green delta

where grass is rich and sweet, and from deep shade
birds call? I think they should not be afraid

to dream, who have so clearly nothing to lose.
But the men, afraid or not, cannot choose

but dream and under each broad demented moon
gather the dream-packets dropped from the balloon.

★

Why am I so sure
they dreamt, although their prison was secure?

Why do I see so clearly
their visions were not idle fancies merely?

Because they live in me.
Behind my eyes what they saw, I still see.

Dream words are spoken
also to me, who by that signal woken

in the cool dawn, cry
as they cried then, *Let me live first, then die,*

not die within
and only then my usefulness begin:

so I am able
to share their dreams in that long cobbled stable.

Able? I have no choice.
They had their patient skills. I have my voice.

★

I

It seems to me at last I should have pride
in finding this horse-marrow in my bones,
in settling down my strength between the traces:
for mine is a horse-world of stone and grass,
I live on horse-patience and horse-desires
and shall pull many loads before I rest.

2

I have lived several lives. Each left its traces.
Less supple now, but not yet out to grass
I feel the morning lyrical in my bones
the light of evening limbers my desires.
To express gratitude is all my pride:
I leave to the winds and waters all the rest.

3

I thank the unknown God who built my bones
and shaped tall colts from mine and their dam's
 desires.
I watch them run. They snort and crop sweet
 grass.
In their young bodies I discern my traces.
They are nerve and sinew. They stamp, and need
 no rest.
All trees and flowers are rooted in my pride.

4

Perhaps when I am taken from the traces
and lay to sleep my time-indentured bones
I shall rise up one day from under grass
dress in new livery my old desires
and this time be a real horse like the rest
not merely a horse of memory and pride.

5

A chestnut, fourteen hands, with all the pride
of silk-fringed hoofs and indestructible bones:
and that human generation who now rest
among forgotten tombstones and long grass
if they could wake, and know the hand that traces
the map of life had willed them new desires,

6

and if the men and horses in their traces
could turn once more to working skill and pride:
O then, if time would grant me my desires
I'd choose to tread, and smell the summer grass,
pulling a narrow-boat. In that thought rest
the fluttering mind, the fever in the bones.

O unknown God who traces my desires,
whose infinite pride can grow through humble
    grass,
make clean my bones with love before I rest!

Thinking About Mr Person

Thinking About Mr Person

Fernando Pessoa (1888–1935), a citizen of Lisbon, wrote four highly
differentiated bodies of poetry, one under his own name (Pessoa, as it
happens, means 'person') and the others under the names Alberto
Caeiro, Ricardo Reis and Alvaro de Campos. A quiet, self-effacing
man who published little, he enjoyed scant reputation in his lifetime,
but is now widely regarded as 'the greatest Portuguese poet since
Camões'.

Alberto Caeiro, Ricardo Reis, Alvaro de Campos,
Fernando Pessoa . . . what resounding Portuguese
      names!

Names full of cloud and seagulls, the surf-crash
of a South-Western coast, the tidal swing of the Tagus:
names full of the weather of Portugal,
the long empty roads, the eucalyptus trees,
the rice fields and the Atlantic promontories:
the sardines grilling over charcoal in side-street bars,
the street-markets, the churches full of God's calm
      shadow,
citizens with head-colds riding in the trams,
the yellow trams of Lisbon.

And the voyagers are in these names, the stern
      Portuguese
who carried Western Europe out over the flashing foam
and the dark waves that dared them, *Come on and drown*,
men with faces of teak, hauling on salt-rimed ropes:
men who carried Western Europe, who carried her,
and carried her, and finally set her down
to become the exiled queen they call Brazil,
the queen who wanders amid strange flowers and
      animals
in a land it would be wrong ever to get used to,
and who is happy because she has lost her memory.

★

Exiled, I called her. But exiles can find home.
Winged seeds can strike root in a far-off soil.
Those Iberian thoughts, those Portuguese
     brain-patterns
became Brazilian. The same, and not the same.
Months of green water: the salt dust on the skin:
till minds faltered: clouds bunched on the horizon
were hailed as mountains, land-smells hallucinated:
at last, the fever of shores that grew clearer,
reached out to receive and save but also to challenge.
And then, the east-facing coast, the different rocks,
the inciting cries of birds without a name.
In that new soil they planted Portugal,
the same, and not the same. The old seeds grew
in a new shape.
                    And Portugal herself
their queen in memory, that light-flooded mist,
drowned in the deep salt water of goodbye.
Encrusted now with dreams, she troubled their sleep
in hammocks slung from tropic boughs, came
     walking
towards them down the avenues of moonlight
regal, smiling, but now not beckoning,
blessing them but no longer calling them back:
she wore her altered vestments of memory
and changed their hearts' rhythm, but only in sleep.

                    ★

These sailors fell in love with the exiled queen
whose thoughts could never be as theirs had been.

Their minds were crazed and opened by the new land:
they needed to love more than to understand.

The earth spoke a new language, the sun, the rain:
the single European focus would never work again.

30

Was Mr Person the heir of that landfall?
Sharing that long stride from singular to plural?

★

Ferns and brambles and long wet stalks of grass
if you're looking for England
you can find bits of her in Portugal
in the pouring mornings of winter
or autumn when the bright dead leaves
stick to the pavements.

Mr Person did not need to look for England:
he carried a little of her inside himself.
He wrote some poems in English.
He often had English thoughts.
He once saw Queen *Victoria*, for God's sake!
It happened in South Africa,
when he was at school in Durban.
What a strange life, a mad history!
But then all our lives are strange, all our
        histories
totally non-credible.

★

Having nuggets of England in his Portuguese mind
must have helped Mr Person to feel less defined

and so less hampered. Rather than to be single
he always found it more rewarding to mingle.

He was the choir-master who invented his choir:
their voices' freedom was his heart's desire.

Leaving the centralizing ego to sink or swim
he made up four poets to shape the world for him:

three had imagined names, one had his own:
this set him free to enjoy being alone.

With three other poets wandering in and out
his mind had plenty to talk to itself about

and he knew that for him it would be a mistake
to inhabit the self-cell with its enclosing ache.

★

What is the self? I cried.
Come, show me where it lives.
What is the coin it gives
to buy my fratricide?

I know that I have brothers
who shyly haunt my dwelling
come when there's no foretelling
depart to solace others:

and sometimes they and I
exchange our names and faces
and walk familiar places
under a changing sky.

One self would keep me tethered
chewing one cud of dreams
forgetting the wild moon-beams
and storms that I have weathered.

Construct a thick-walled tower
and seal it with a name
the tower will stay the same
but the name lose its power.

Be singular, be one
deny the spirit's flowing
in dying or in growing
brook no companion

and find when night comes down
you journeyed round and round
a barren patch of ground
not moved through field and town.

The poet eyed the key
that turned in the self's door
eyed ceiling, walls and floor
askance, distrustfully

wanting no final choice
of mask or diagram
no sealed-in 'this I am':
needing his plural voice.

★

He welcomed life, Mr Person. Let us give her a capital
    letter:
loved and responded to Life, and when she put in an
    appearance
was always happy to greet her, and kept his room dusted
    on purpose
to welcome the goddess – but never grappled or tried to
    detain her.
Some men act as if Life were a girl they were keen to shack
    up with –
making traps, laying bait, showing off when they know
    she can see them.
Mr Person, for his part, treated life more like a neighbour:
since she was never far off, he could count on meeting her
    sometimes.
Often they talked in the street, conversation without any
    forethought,
sometimes she dropped in to see him, and then they spent
    longer in contact
she being guest, he host, their relationship felt as more
    structured,
then again to the smile in the hallway, the five minutes'
    talk at the bus-stop.
Mr Person's ambition was simply that Life should accept
    him

; a presence without demands, a lover not seeking to own
  her:
almly, reliably there, till the day when his coffin was
  called for.

★

Mr Person liked to think of rivers. Water flowing
in its own channel was his emblem of knowing:
his life and art, a breathing and a bestowing.

He liked truths that find their way with no resistance
and nature that is peaceful in her own existence.
He distrusted clever proofs and loud-voiced insistence.

To Mr Person, a river making its way decently
and without fuss to the inevitable sea
cradling quiet fish and algae, was the thing to be.

He spoke often of rivers, how they seldom died.
To him they were the pure logic. Often I sit beside
a river and think of Mr Person with a quiet pride.

★

Since Mr Person accepted the world so tranquilly
he foresaw the possibility of someone like me

moved for various reasons to think of him
on clear mornings or nightfall soft and dim

since he saw no particular reason for anything
he would accept that I sometimes need to laugh and sing

when I think of him, and besides there is the fact
that we share our love of the earth like a secret pact.

Soft Portuguese distances of hazy green
hazy distances of England where my life has been

silver and green of the olive, silver and green of the
  willow
these are the gentlest colours I shall ever know

34

waves rolling in to shore, birds walking on the sand
I am rooted and calm in Portugal as in England

these sloping sea-misted lands with their salt breath
to love them both is part of my natural faith

they exist in the cry of the Atlantic gull
and I shall always find them alive and beautiful.

Enobarbus

Enobarbus

I'm grizzled now. A skull packed with memories.
When I was young, if anyone had said
Where does your strength come from? I'd have laughed.
Where does anything's strength come from? Shoots
push from the warm earth: even desert sand,
given one shower of rain, grows green with seed
that must have been hiding somewhere.
                                               Frogs
leap twelve times their own length, birds climb the wind,
the lion rips open the gazelle's hot flank.
And I, Enobarbus, Red-beard,
have shoulders to support plated armour
a spine to stand upright with a loaded pack,
legs hard for the Alpine passes, a hand
that can squeeze a man's life out of his throat
if his studded shield has broken my sword.
Sea and the rocks are strong. I am strong.
Soldier-strong, Enobarbus-strong:
a man born to lift armies off the earth
and press them backwards to surrender and death:
that's what I'd have said.

                All strength comes from the sun. I knew that.
                But I had not learnt
                what it means to know that.

                All strength reaches down
                from
                the gold-bossed, impersonal
                all-giving, staring, unrecognising
                indifferent
                sun.

                The sun that warms
                carrion for maggots

burnishes the dead moon
tortures to death the lost
soldier in the desert
tunes the throats of birds
in February

the sun
the sun
this I had not yet learnt:

till I saw Antony.

After that
I saw the oak-tree's strength
locked in the acorn.

Only the son has the key.

Only the sun has my key.

★

Everyone said he was like Hercules.
What is it for a man to be like a god?

Gods are all round us, like air.

they are under our feet, like earth.

we drink them, we breathe them, we
hear them, we know them:
we forget them like the things we know best.

We eat them
so their strength becomes ours
it is the only strength we have

gods have long green limbs
and flowers for faces
and gesturing leaves for hands

gods have heads of spray

and smooth dimpled skin
rock-rounding

gods have rough pelts
and bucking horns
and genitals of flame

gods have
gods have

and sometimes they give it
sometimes
to one of us

★

That winter when he took us through the Alps . . .

Enobarbus remembers the Alps

The mountains never think of death. Or life.
Their huge white heads are turned the other way,
their sharp stone teeth bared to the sharper air.

He carries full pack and spear
like the rest of us. His shoes
squeak on the snow like ours.
That's in the morning, when
we start to climb. By noon
the sun glares from hot blue: we're frying
in our own grease. His shield
throws back hard yellow at the sun.
For God's sake rest the men.
They're starving: some are struck with
snow-blindness, have to put their hands
on the others' shoulders.
                              Suck ice,
he says, it will at least
fill your stomachs with clean water.
And march.

Snow-heads that cannot think of death are turned

away from life. Huge teeth grin at the sky.
They can not care. They can not know. Can not.

March. Suck ice. There will
be rations waiting on
the downward side. Two days.
It is forbidden to die
before then. Suck ice. March.

The snow squeaks in the morning. Later
it is slush. Laden men splash
and slip. When the sun goes
behind those snow-heads and stone
teeth, the night will pounce. We
shall be loaded with skin-peeling
chains of ice.
                A goat's bones
lie scattered. It must have starved,
weakened, and fallen kicking
from a crag. Its burst
skeleton, cleaned white by crows,
lies close by our path. Everyone
sees it. Everyone thinks
of his own weakening, his own
fall, his own wrecked skeleton.
Nobody speaks, nobody wants
to hear his own voice say
'starvation' or 'goat'.

And that thing he ate!
It must have been the corpse of
a marmot, or something.
The smell made me puke.
But he ate it, standing up:
'I must have strength,' he said calmly.

That's how he went through the Alps.
That's how he went through battles.
That's how he went through women.
            ★

Cleopatra? Yes, very beautiful.
Did I what?
                    Well, of course,
I know the answer you're expecting.
But funnily enough, no, I didn't
fantasize about her.
                    I followed
him around, in most things, but
not that far.
                    Whenever
he was in there, after dinner, undressing her,
getting up to all those tricks (the slaves
used to spy on them, we all
knew everything): even on those hot nights
when I would lie in my tent, feeling
randy enough for anything, sweating,
trying not to masturbate because
I wanted to be fresh next day, even then:
no.
           It's as if my body knew
she was for him, not me.
Oh, she was every bit as beautiful
as they say. And *une grande
horizontale*. Look, I know sex
when I see it. Yet what burned in her
wasn't just sex. It was that and
something else.
                    What else? Well,
I can't find words for it. You know those fish
with a phosphorescent spine? This – something – lit
      her up
all through her shape, like that.
                                   To Antony,
she was just another woman in the end.
That's because his magic equalled hers.
To me, she was always music, a dance,
colour, a skin of wine, the seasons

43

on a base of woman.
                    And sex? That big
erection she's supposed to have given the men
just by walking past?
                    I don't care
whether you believe or not, I never
had it.
                    And yet, well
what I felt for her was never chaste:
it was close to lust. Close to it, but different.
I don't know how to put it. I would have liked
to do something to her, something bold
and very intimate, yet not quite sexual:
such as, for instance, licking her armpits.

Yes, that would have satisfied me.
Or driven me mad for ever. Enough now.

                    ★

Cleopatra was

the red vein in a smooth
white pebble

Cleopatra was

a voice from down among the cluster
of houses by the waterfront

singing the same song
over and over

on one of those nights when you can't sleep
a song with the richness of tears

Cleopatra was

a hot jet of goat-sperm

Cleopatra was

a winged seed fluttering down,

44

taking a long time to reach the ground

Cleopatra was

the lace of cloud that moves
past the staring moon

Cleopatra was

the sparkle of salt on the stiff ropes
of a fishing boat

when it rests in the sun, and the men
who fought the sea's fury, rest
in the calm of the sun, and drink wine

Cleopatra
           was

★

In the brief dusk they heard it
when swallows wheel
for the last time before resting
for the last time before their quick heart-beat
composes to sleep
in cups of mud and straw
still beating fast in sleep
but not caring, not seeking, not needing, quiet
in the warmth of clay and stone:

in the brief dusk
when the sky turns cool
when the light turns green:
in the silent time
before the frogs in the hot night
before the owls
before the long yell of the wild dog
before the song from the taverns:
as the swallows wheel for the last time
the soldiers heard it:

his music of desolation.
They listened and fear struck them
they listened and sorrow bowed their heads
they listened and could not speak.

Later, pale and quiet-voiced
they told us of it:

the music under the ground
in the motionless air
among the tranced limbs of trees
the music of desolation:
the good-bye music.

What god left him?
Hercules, king of war
or Bacchus, ruler of feasts?
they asked each other.
What god loved him most?

In the brief dusk
they were afraid of the green light.

Who cares what god left him?
It was music of ending:
the lithe wings folding back,
the rustle of their closing.

When a man's luck gives out
he hears that music in his skull
in the brief dusk:
who cares what god makes it?

No more of questions and answers.
The great sun drops down.
The swallows have nested.

★

Enobarbus reasons with Subrabone
    I lie here in the soft, stifling darkness

staring straight up at the roof of my tent.
Rain is falling. The ropes should be slackened.

Enobarbus

Look, try to understand. Soldiering is a profession. You
don't open a shop with nothing to sell. And you don't
write a book nobody is going to read. Unless you're
mad.
And I'm not mad. The only point of fighting is to win.
Striking attitudes, making fine speeches, throwing your
life away, they're for amateurs.

Subrabone

If it is over, strike your tent and move.
He has nothing to hold you but the chains of love.

Enobarbus

He can't win. His luck has run out. Not that I really
believe in luck: that's the point. A professional knows
how to stay sane. He weighs the chances and goes in at
the right time, in the right place, with the right men and
equipment or else he doesn't go in at all.

Subrabone

You think it folly to have served so long?
A great defeat can ring like a great song.

Enobarbus

He's a madman. That's what she's made of him. Every-
one
who was there knows I tried my best. I knew if someone
didn't pry him loose from her he'd sooner or later be a
dead duck. Well, now it's happened. He's finished.

Subrabone

It is not your small thoughts make you
    faint-hearted
but that still music as the loved god departed.

Enobarbus

He's finished but is that any reason why I should be
finished with him? Where's the sense in that, where's
the justice? It's not as if I were betraying my country.
This is a quarrel between Romans. A sane Roman against
a mad Roman. All I'm doing is crossing the lines from
Roman to Roman, from the mad to the sane, it's my
duty. An experienced soldier is an asset to the Empire.
If I stay with Antony I'll be as much use as a slaughtered
pig hanging up beside a stall with a hook through one
foot. Not even that much use because I'm no good to
eat. I'd be no prettier to look at and I'd be just as dead.

Rain, rain. Where's my orderly? Asleep
or drunk? The ropes should be slackened, fool,
the ropes should be slackened. The ropes
should be slackened.

★

And now at last I am
alone in my nerve-ends

unable to call his name
or any name

houseless, a sound
'Enobarbus'

no self, no possibility
of touching another

and now at last I am
insubstantial

my suchness
blown to a mist

tales of my courage
a scarf of mist

48

ENOBARBUS

my Jove-scattering sex
mist over the ditched fields

smoke from a guttering candle
in a socket of solitude

and now at last I am
and now at last
and now
and

Poem for Kids

Poem for Kids

An old, old man lived down our street
as old as a tortoise with leathery feet

as old as a carp or a minstrel's harp
his eyes were dim but his wits were sharp

he sat and watched the years go by
(perhaps he just *forgot* to die)

he sat and watched the suns go down
no one remembered when his hair was brown

(perhaps it was already white
when Waterloo-men went to fight

perhaps it was as white as frost
when Flodden field was won and lost).

I used to think he was as old
as the first drinking-cups of gold

but his memories lay where they were stored
and he loved the world and he never got bored

and every night when he sank to rest
his dreams were rich, his dreams were blest.

I sometimes wondered why he seemed
so glad with whatever it was he dreamed

and I asked him once, what his dreams were
        made of?
he answered, *Nothing to be afraid of:*

Just memories of long-gone days
when the world moved in different ways,

just memories of things long gone:
they have passed, but I live on,

and so in the dreams inside my head
they will have a home till I am dead.

And I asked him once if he'd rather be
back when the world moved differently:

I asked him once, but all he would say
was, *Some things go and some things stay,*
and the world is a new world every day.

★

This old man had worked on a ship
and watched the billows swing and skip

in the days when ships held out their sails
to catch the breezes, to dare the gales,

when the engine-room was the windy sky
and the ship drove on with her mast held high

or the ship stood still and the sails hung idle
and skipper and mate were suicidal

till the first sail swelled and the first rope stirred
and the ship came alive like a waking bird:

and there was no coal and there was no oil
just the wind and compass and seamen's toil

and there was no stain and there was no scum
in the harbours where the cargoes come

no dead birds with useless wings
washed up by the tide like forgotten things

only the shove of the salt-sea air
and the cold white horses galloping there.

And I often wondered if he longed to be
afloat again on that sparkling sea

back in those clean and salty days
before the slicks and the greasy haze:

I asked him once, but all he would say,
was, *Some things go and some things stay,*
and the world is a new world every day.

★

Then one day, just before he died,
he took my arm, drew me aside:

yes, just before his spirit passed
he must have thought he'd talk at last.

When I was born I don't remember
but from January to December

in every year that has gone round
since the first man walked on the ground

things were that should never have been
and sights you'd rather not have seen.

No words can ever tell man's story
without some shame, without some glory:

if you go back a thousand years
the picture neither clouds nor clears.

Our kindly earth was not so spoiled,
yet some men lazed, and some men toiled:

some men laughed and some men groaned
and one looked on while another was stoned:

yet there was goodness, too, and boldness,
to set against the greed and coldness.

It's one long tale, without a sequel
and its bad and its good are just about equal:

so what I have to say, young man,
is, Laugh and sing as much as you can:

for some things go, and some things stay,
and the world is a new world every day!

Deor

Deor

from the Anglo-Saxon

Among snake-patterned swords | Weland tasted
   sorrow
noble in mind | he knew misery
yearning and loss | he lived alongside
winter-cold wandering. | Woe he found
when Nithhad cramped him |with well-contrived
fetters for his sinews | the finer man.
That passed. So may this of mine.

To Beadohild the death | of her brother even
was not so pitiful | as her own plight
when beyond doubt | she was driven
to know herself with child. | Never cheerfully
could she abide the thought | of that birth-bringing.
That passed. So may this of mine.

We have heard | how Meathhild's heart-grief
Geat's wife | grew beyond measuring.
Love's sorrow stole | from her all sleep.
That passed. So may this of mine.

Theodoric held down | through thirty winters
the town of the Mearings: | many marked it.
That passed. So may this of mine.

We know the evil | name of Eormanric
he of wolf's mind, | who worked his will
on Gothic ground. | That was a grim king.
Many a man | endured misery
inured to woe | hoping always
that his dominion | might be dashed down.
That passed. So may this of mine.

The rueful man | robbed of joy's rites
abides in darkness: | doom, he decides,

wills that his end | be woe for ever.
But let him think | all through this world
wise God chooses | to bring unceasing change:
to many a man | he shows mercy,
assured success: | and to some, sorrow.

I will speak now | of my own state:
honoured beforetime | as bard of the Heodenings,
dear to my lord. | They called me Deor.
For many winters | it was well with me
in my lord's loyalty, | until lately
Heorrenda skilful in song | was steaded
with the land | my lord allotted me.
That passed. So may this of mine.

Shorter Poems

1970–1978

'Your beauty chokes me.
Colour, shape, all'

Your beauty chokes me. Colour, shape, all.
But chokes me into peace. My conflicts die
Like clouds that shred into a perfect sky.

I hope yours do the same, who give so much.
One truth at least I know: when we lie down
You shiver into pleasure at my touch.

I never can deserve you: still, I try.
What can I give you, but this Bacchanal?
The bill is waiting, and we must go Dutch.

But oh the radiant smile behind time's frown!

Oh forest where the flimsy shoots grow tall!
Oh clean and salty ocean where we drown!

Song of the Far Places

Before I saw any of the postcard places
I lived among Staffordshire names and faces

before I knew where the warm Gulf Stream went
I staged twig-races on the sickly infant Trent

I read of Mississippi bayou, fjord, calanque
and I watched the wind-stirred water from the canal
    bank

dreaming of wildebeeste and voortrekker
I went voyaging on a Potteries double-decker

reckoning up sheikdom and emirate
I cycled to Woore, Black Brook and Pipe Gate.

They told me tales of antarctic and equator
and the broad snout of the questing alligator

afloat on jungle rivers, Orinoko and Amazon
and I watched the canal water grow dark as damson

and the turquoise dragon-flies hover and disappear:
the black tips fumed but nature was always near.

The pylons marched overhead but the long grass
    waved
nothing in nature was tidy or well-behaved:

I had not seen the Alps in spring blue with gentians
but I watched hedgerow lovers with their warm
    intentions

and though the males were hot-blooded in Brindisi
among ferns in Trentham Park they had it just as easy

and if girls were submissive in Japan and Korea
in nettle-green alleys between Longton and the Meir

they showed no more sign of prudish alarm
than their stark-naked sisters in Dar-es-Salaam.

Before I saw any of the postcard sights
I heard the loud cold wind on winter nights

throwing tiles off roofs and slashing at the trees
roaring in Penkhull as it roared in the Hebrides

and in the long summer when the baked soil hardens
the winged seeds came floating over the back gardens

teaching me what the earth is like in the burnt south
where spring water is sweeter than kisses to the
    mouth

for Hanley Deep Pit seemed ready to throw up lava
Trent Vale and Hanford were tropical as Java.

Yes, before I saw any of the postcard views
I knew the richness of land and water was mine to
    choose

which parts excited or lulled or frighteningly chilled
    me
and pierced my marrow with beauty or in dreams
    fulfilled me.

The hymnody of the earth is the same for you and for
    me,
which means childhood is the same wherever you
    happen to be,
except in a high-rise apartment with a colour TV.

65

Czech Students in Oxford,
Seen Across a Room, 1968

It is always summer in his dream of home:
the wheat scarcely ripe, and the swallows
coming in low for insects.

That was the summer of the brimming river
when the grasshoppers chirped like choristers:
vespers and matins in a new dialect!

Now, home is a tangle of roots.

Now, he wakes to the dark mornings.
Frost has made hardware of the earth:
its veins cold as the forgetful tracks of tanks.

Fall, snow, fall, weightless snow
from the mothering sky:
conceal the biding roots where life is gathered,
the rune-dark roots whose names are his only prayers.

To My Young Self

I remember you so well, lank-haired restless one.
Shall we attempt a dialogue at last?

If I could roll up three decades like a worn carpet,
and walk with you among these trees,

or in this lane by the old blackened wall,
where your starveling footstep often came,

among these scenes that keep the same outline,
it might calm both of us.

After all, we came through it together,
you changing slowly into me.

Came through what? Ah, diablotin,
we both know how jagged was the path

and how our joint footfall altered its nature:
becoming heavier, more poised, less free.

You wandered in a hailstorm of choices,
each choice numbered and coloured like snooker.

Decisions, choices, possibilities,
rolling on the green cloth of your life.

One by one they disappeared into pockets:
now only a few are left to invite collision.

I chalk my cue for the shots that will decide the
    game.
I need skill, where you needed only appetite.

Cadaverous joker, the feelings that shook your
    bones
and broke your health, were in fact your best
    friends.

Your voice echoed among Easter Island heads:
mine shouts along a valley littered with broken
    waxworks.

You had to break iron bars to get out:
I have to unpick silken ropes to stay out.

Nothing could help you but the stubbornness to
  live.
Nothing can help me but the stubbornness to live.

The word led you upward into a mountain
  landscape.
The word leads me downward to the banks of a
  strong river.

You were in danger of falling and being broken.
I am in danger of sinking and being engulfed.

But after all, we are the same person, gallowglass,
both the same timorous but untrainable animal:

more easy under the cold sky than in a kennel,
rooting for bitter grubs, not waiting to be fed
  mince.

You with the wild laughter and the apprehensive
  eyes,
wondering where the next smash on the nose
  would come from:

I, knowing by this time just where it will come
  from:
no longer laughing like a madman, my eyes calmer.

Well, I have enjoyed our talk together,
though I admit I did most of the talking

and found it rather difficult to draw you out:
but then I am fifty-one, and you are what? twenty?

twenty-one, twenty-five? in any case, bambino,
though I do not suppose you trust me, I will trust
  you,

having not much else to trust, and no patrimony
save the few battered belongings that used to be
  yours.

'Outside, gulls squabbled in the empty street'

Outside, gulls squabbled in the empty street. Criticism
and name-calling. Salt air scrubbed the gleaming
Sunday morning walls. Gutter-split stalks, leaves, fuelled the
    squalling
and wheeling. Feet, motors, slept. The inured citizens
turned over to snore again. Beside me, my darling

slept in a deeper peace, like a princess in a fable
all through the sea-clean, gull-torn dawn, slept below
    dreaming,
stunned by those hours of outrageous bliss, bliss upon bliss,
when love leapt higher than even the fiercest lovers were able.
Patient, I lay, expecting tea and her morning kiss.

At Jowett's Grave

Majestic he sailed,
flagship of a navy
sails puffed with every wind
that pride could summon.

They were going to *rule*:
to command, to direct, to prescribe,
to categorize, to set in order:

and always with his eye on them.
And damn it, they *did* all those things,
and always with his eye on them.
Never apologise, never explain!
And they never did.

So majestic he sailed
until at last he docked by these flat stones,
got out of his high painted ship, and lay down.

Lay down in sour earth
with nettles, docks and mares' tails
amid the cut-price comforts of small lives
in a graveyard no bigger than a tennis court.

And it is all there today,
for the small lives persist like the mares' tails
(common and beautiful as the veined wings of flies)
and will have their cut-price
comforts and conveniences,
the dock-leaves to assuage their endless nettles:
small pubs, small shops, a factory where they work,
off-licence, fish and chips, a laundromat.

While a few streets away, in the same rooms
where he lived out his life, the port goes round,
the talk goes on, the truths are shredded out
and the points scored, with stroke and
            counter-stroke
('That was damned bad sherry you gave us, Master,

if it comes to that,' and it still does come to that):
and he lies in unsunned earth, almost near enough
to catch what they are saying, and join in,
but for the little accident of death.

There is no memorial: I stumbled
on his grave by chance one day,
waiting for my wife to have a baby
in the hospital down the road.
(You were the baby, Toby, and I want
you to accept this poem, if you will –
not that I want you to grow up like Jowett.)

And yet a man could do worse,
worse I mean than grow up like Jowett:
and much, much worse than lie like him in death.

Shaded by the factory wall he lies,
among the docks and nettles and mares' tails:
his navy sunk, his ship burnt long ago:

a candidate for elegy, but not pity.
He is still there, strong in six feet of earth:

secure in the overhead flight of swans
that make the air hiss through their heavy pinions:
in the embrace of earth, the nearness of water,
the cheerful stubbornness of the springing weeds –

still not apologising, never explaining.

Evening over the Place of Cadfan

Over again, these gifts: the high bareness:
the spear-grass, the sheep carved in stone
watching me pass, the darkening granite
still dabbed with lyric green. And at my back
the levelled-off tips dead quiet, these man-made cliffs
too surgical for grass, human work to the end,
but work of departed giants, all that determination
signed off for ever, the hubbub of silenced voices:
after such purpose, nothing but loneliness, wildness:
and out at sea,
the day's sun in his lead coffin.

Rhosgadfan, Gwynedd
1975

Performers

Tensed, flexing, they make the leap.
Notion to enactment. Flesh gathered to a purpose
outside its own needs, yet fuelled by them.
Bruised, always ready to be bruised again:
and cherished, suckled, dreaming within a dream
of another dream, never-ending, lit from within,
a dream small enough to swallow like a pill,
big enough to wander in hand in hand
with everyone you ever loved, where the present
moment never comes to an end. This is
surely what they are searching for. Look at their eyes.
The dream within the dream: it has to be that.

The trance-state must be catching: normally I
feel my mind realistic, ballasted. Now
among them, I feel less sure. Outlines flicker.
Flat shorelines become thickets of dark-green weed.
A mountain fades into cold white smoke, then becomes
a cloud that hardens into snow. Then thaws.
Let's pretend. And now we've finished pretending,
let's pretend that what we're doing now is real.
And if it isn't real, let's still pretend.
Ought I to resist? They confuse me, but gladly
I embrace confusion. Their petulant moments,
even, are a sharp game I relish. Why?
What spell do they put on me? It must be
the deep assent they give to transformation.
Their openness is beyond morality.
To take so readily might just as well be to give:
take, give: take, give: the words change places
till one tires of watching: do a swallow's wings
take from the wind, or offer themselves to it?
Their egotism is a sacrifice
of self. I breathe the pyre's sky-climbing plume.
So the cardboard turns out to be rock, the paints
are really the true colours of nature.
That girl's feigned tears fall for all slow griefs.

To simulate passion is to remember it,
to remember passion is to invite more:
watching them pretend, I become more real:
their rehearsed movements unlock my limbs to freedom.

So ritual makes hard truth into a dream
that could come true. And as Imagination,
the red-nosed clown, squirts from his button-hole,
true laughter rises up, true tears run down.

Blind Man Listening to Radio

I

Gold and silver carp
nose to the surface
of the flat pool. Lily stems
trail through my fingers.
The fish have cool, round
invented voices.

II

Pacing my dark brown oblong
I touch the shiny black wood
of a clarinet. The air
grows suddenly sweeter.

III

I nest like a mouse
in the folds of a great newspaper.
With a rustle of pages
I settle my back and shoulders,
ready for conversation.

IV

It is morning. The smell of coffee
and the announcer's calm voice,
telling of bombs and murder.

V

A pot of black peat. Seeds
rain in. Quickly, a flower grows.
Another. Then another.

VI

A woman's voice
warmed in a soft throat.

I think of her rounded body
tense, on the studio chair.

VII

I lie in bed, twirl a serrated knob.
From my ear, a beam goes out
across oceans, continents. I taste the crash of surf,
the wind in the gull's pinions,
the hard feet of mules in the high passes.

On a Beautiful Girl who Loved the Wrong Man

On this pile of dry and twisted sticks
old leaves and dust, the dove cannot alight.

You thought to bring moss, to plump out
a round space for love, to shield with feathers.

You gave him the blessing of your close breathing,
you sucked out his black humours.

How could he touch your skin and not sing tuneful praises?
Where were the cymbals and trumpets?

That he could bathe in your spring and still come out
    parched!
Truly the Maker of men went strangely to work.

You searched for him in his own labyrinth:
every path ran out into thorns and dust.

Your heart understands only love and acceptance.
Finding a toad, you see only his jewelled eye.

You looked for a jewel and you found one,
lying on faded velvet in a locked showcase.

That he should read love in your eyes, and in the braille of
    your nipples,
and render as tribute such dry and such bitter seeds!

Stand away from his side, girl! The sultry weather is
    coming,
when he will certainly be struck by lightning!

My Name

*(If I lived in a culture whose poets take bardic names,
I would choose to be called Flying-fish.)*

Flying-fish loves the salt kiss of brine:
Flying-fish loves the leap into slanting air.

Flying-fish loves the bottle-green of the depths:
his soul expands in the diminishing light.

Flying-fish fears the dry smack of a deck-landing:
Flying-fish fears the ring of grinning captors.

Most of all he abhors the poison-droolers:
the vomit of selfishness, the sea's foul overcoat.

Flying-fish loves the long rhythms of the swell,
he has patience with its settle and swing, settle and
        swing.

Flying-fish fears the slyness of net and trawl,
he grieves for his brothers who thrash in that stricture.

Flying-fish offers his sperm to the smooth scales of a
        mate:
he loves to come close amid the vastness of ocean.

Flying-fish fears the bleep of sonic detectors:
to escape technology, he flashes through air and foam.

Flying-fish is nourished by the marrow of colours,
a rainbow fattens him like a wedding-breakfast.

Flying-fish does not fear death.
Night is friendly to him, and death is night:

calm night on the ocean, with uncountable stars,
and fragrances blowing off the islands.

Flying-fish does not fear death.
But he loves life: he is in no hurry

to resign motion, to float with stiffened fins,
to be part of the sea's phosphorescent detritus.

When the time comes, he will accept night:
meanwhile each morning and evening he splashes and
   glides,

in search of more life, singing in water-language:
More, more, more, always let there be more!

'You dropped me, at high speed.
Some skin tore off'

You dropped me, at high speed. Some skin tore off,
then grew again. I climbed out of that trough.
Yet still I thought, how beautiful you were.

The winter passed, sullen with rags of ice.
Spring, summer. I felt happy, once or twice.
Yet still it burnt, how beautiful you were.

One hot day, I was riding in a train.
I knew that we would never meet again.
Though it ticked on, how beautiful you were.

I had a long and boring way to go:
I slumped and sweated, trying to read Malraux.
And not to think how beautiful you were.

Whenever you rose to my conscious mind
I kept my thoughts forgiving, wise and kind.
For after all, how beautiful you were.

So much a moon, so cool and uninvolved:
a love avoided was a problem solved.
Yet still and all, how beautiful you were.

You had no needs. You neither took nor gave.
How else should ice and emerald behave?
Dumbly I stared. How beautiful you were.

The train was slowing. Idly I glanced out.
And then my nerves began to twitch and shout.
Because they knew how beautiful you were.

This was your town: your sun, your sky, your air!
I had not reckoned on our stopping there:
reckoning only, how beautiful you were.

The train ran smoothly past the streets. I eyed
the neat front doors, the shiny cars outside.
They must have known how beautiful you were.

Did one of those tiled roofs keep rain from you?
Were you close by? The longing ran me through
with a bright blade. How beautiful you were.

I only knew that somewhere in this town
you had your rising up and lying down.
In all you did, how beautiful you were.

The platform slid alongside, then stood still.
I tried to fight the pain by strength of will.
The pain. Because how beautiful you were.

At last we started. Slowly, then more fast,
walls, bridges, some more streets, went healing
        past.
Back there. Lost now. How beautiful you were.

I surfaced from those depths wherein I dived.
The green fields came again. I had survived.
Even though I knew how beautiful you were.

I breathed relief. But as I drew that sigh
I saw your image printed on the sky.
With no clothes on, how beautiful you were!

On a Tree Cut in Paper

Time went backwards:
the toothed wheel screamed in the fibres
dust sprayed in the bewildering air
the rings parted in sorrow,
the trunk floated downstream.
                                    Then,
worlds later, under light bulbs
the wet street outside the pane
where avid machines snorted and time
slid sideways on smoke and spoiling,

in a quiet room, the scissors
torn with the same anguish, the same
impatience from wounded rockwomb, made
precise cuts that spoke of love;

love for leaves, twigs,
roots, bark, berries; all
the betrayed, the forgotten angels –
the grains, the streams, the nests.

'Know Thyself'

a translation into English alliterative metre
of the Latin hexameters written by Samuel Johnson
on completing his revision of the Dictionary, 1772

Scaliger, when with scant sense of achievement he had scrawled
his lexicon's last page, after prolonged toil, loathing
the mindless menial grind, the small problems piled into
    mountains,
in hate groaning, he gave his thought to guide grave judges
that the penal system should prescribe for all hard prisoners
found guilty of devilment, the drudgery of making a dictionary –
one punishment, for the most impenitent, all punishments
    compounding!

How right he was, that rare man, erudite, lofty, rigorous,
worthy of weightier work, better able to serve the world
by enchanting the ear with antique heroisms, or the bards'
    ecstasies,
the shifting sands of governance, the swirl of the shining spheres
his mind could read and unriddle, and the vast earth's revolving.

A large example is dangerous. The dunciad of learned dolts
glare and grumble, presenting their case, princely Scaliger
as if it were yours, master. Let each mind his measure!
I, at least, have realized that to be your rival (in rage
or in knowledge) was never part of my nature. Who can know
    why?
Is it the lazy flow of my chill blood, or the long idle years
    that I lost?
Or was I just bundled into the world with a bad brain?

As soon as your sterile work was over, and the stiff
    word-stubble
you had pushed through, peerless wisdom the goddess into her
    pure
arcanum accepted you, while all the arts applauded,
and the world's words, their voices so long at variance,
now home from exile joyfully rang about you, gentle master,
    their joiner.

As for me, my task finished, I find myself still fettered to myself:
the dull doom of doing nothing, harsher than any drudgery,
stays with me, and the staleness of slow stagnation.
Cares beget cares, and a clamouring crowd of troubles
vex me, and vile dreams, the sour sleep of an empty mind.
What will refresh me? The rattle of all-night roisterers,
or the quiet of solitary spaces? Oh, sleep, sleep, I call,
lying where I fret at the lingering night, but fear day's cold
    finger.
Trembling, I trudge everywhere, peering, prying, into
    everything, trying
passionate to know if somewhere, anyhow, a path leads up to a
    more perfect pasture
but glooming over grand schemes I never find my
    growing-point,
and am always forced finally to face myself, to own frankly
that my heart is illiterate, and my mind's strength an illusion
I labour to keep alive. Fool, a mind not fuelled by learning
slides into a morass. Stop the supply of marble
to Phidias our fertile sculptor, and where are his forms and
    faces?
Every endeavour, every avenue, ends in frustration always,
closed in by lack of cash, bound up by a costive mind.
Ah, when that mind reckons up its resources, the harvest of
    reasoning
stacked high, matter for self-satisfaction, is conspicuously absent:
nor does creation's great king from his high castle
send down daily supplies to ensure its survival.
Regularly the years mount up, regularly the mind's works do
    not mount up:
as for the frills and the friendly honours, fruits of a useful life,
its own harsh judgement forbids it that harmless enjoyment.
Turning to survey its territory, that night-shadowed tundra,
the mind is full of fear – of ghosts, of the fleeting gleam
of the thin shadows of nothing, the absence of shapes, the
    shimmer.

What then am I to do? Let my declining years go down to the
   dark?
Or get myself together, gather the last of my gall,
and hurl myself at some task huge enough for a hero?

And if that's too much, perhaps my friends might find me
some dull, decent job, undemanding: like making a
   dictionary . . .

In the Beginning

Now, in our perfect hour,
while the green stem supports the weightless
    flower,
before the rains, before the blurring mist
disturb the globe of silence where we kissed,
let us be calm and tranquil in its power.

There may be love
as daily and enduring as a glove:
this may be granted when perfection fades,
but never the silken magic that pervades
this first fine tapestry our fingers wove.

Your beauty lifts my heart
to a dimension where time has no part.
It must come down, I know: we take our places
among the normal names and normal faces:
but not in these first hours, not from
    the start.

This equilibrium,
most rare and perilous balance, leaves me dumb
to say it all, to name the gems and metals
(flame of a butterfly before it settles)
before the troubles and the questionings come.

Before our ship is tested,
before we sail where seas are cold and crested,
for this one hour let lust be pure as laughter:
let your love breathe without before and after,
soft as the hollow where a bird has rested.

From

Letters To Five Artists

(1969)

Introductory Poem

*addressed to all the friends to whom
these Poems are written:
about Exile, and a Roman Poet on a Ship,
and a Modern Poet at an Airport,
and Red Indians, and Horsemen on the Ice,
and a Boy in 1900*

The salt wind carries no land-smells. Even
the birds have gone back. Indifferent, they
scream on the cliffs, watch for the next boat
setting out.
                    Now the world is water.
Soil must have fed these timbers long ago,
when I had no name. Now those packed grains
root-sheltering, calm, warmed with Italian sun
are a memory. Their world, like mine, is the waves
the bearded rocks far under the waves, and the
            monsters
our minds cannot guess at, waiting there.

Even my mind?

                    So fed with prodigies,
instructed in the suddenness of change,
beast's head, arms of a shrub? A girl's
smooth-running limbs turned to a sliding stream?

Even now, cast out, shamed, it is the same mind,
made nimble by leaping among prodigies:

I, if anyone, could name the unnamed who swim
mindlessly waiting in their salty gloom?
No. I fear them too much. Water changes all.

I, lover of women, those swelling gourds,
I, devotee of liquefaction: shape
dissolved in shape, stiff blood-crammed pleasure
dissolved in warmth and wetness: I, the singer
of change and melting, the lazy river

89

of pleasure winding through the seasons,
the girls new-named, new-faced, but always the same
  girl:
I, now, to learn about water!
       To hear the creak
of the strained ropes, the loud complaint
of timbers sawn from their green and changing trees,
planed, caulked, sent floating far from the smell of
  land:

to lie on this wooden bunk, lonely and sick
and hear the merciless waves drum on the hull
telling me:
    this, after all, is the nature of water!

The baby floats in a living pond:
       The grown man
thirsts for the eager juice of a ripe girl.
Wetness, wetness!
      fountains in the dusty squares,
the quick live jet that danced in the dry air,
the splash and cool drip over the stone lip,
like love, like easy love:
haunches and breasts like ripe halves of a peach!
Now water prods and slaps me purple. Deep
in its belly the empty-eyed
monsters hide.
     Was this always
true? Did water breed monsters, predatory
teeth honed for a poet's flesh,
from the beginning?
Ars Amatoria. That thirst undid me.
I changed. I wrote of change. Of how
life danced, and danced, and never would be still.
This, too, was thirst: was thirst for the same drink,
for heat and liquid change liquid and heat,
men alter girls, girls change the lives of men:

but still the dusty throat
cried thirst, and only thirst, chewed my dry lines
and drank the salty juice, and cried more thirst,

and after nine years the unreachable man
with a god's mask, took from a slave's hand
his golden stylus and wrote down my name,
snapped shut the blazing jewel-case of Rome
with me outside, crying, for ever outside.

Liquid, liquid undid me.
                    Washed, floated
away out of memory. Soft girls
trapped my thoughts hard. These waves
can beat timber to a pulp.
                    To learn about water . . .

Publius Ovidius Naso, this is you!

You, and not only you. The poet's flesh
is always divided and swallowed among whispers.
Whisper of grain on grain, of undersea
siftings, of ritual enacted without passion,
enacted so that the channel shall stay open
to belief, to passion, to the trembling FIAT.

You, Ovidius, and not only you, are exiled.

BOAC announce the departure of their flight
whateveritis
will passengers for this flight please
go to the top of the main staircase

See him rise from his nervous seat
flight-bag and magazines clutched in his hand
stomach already soothed with Dramamine
Dogrose, the poet in a drip-dry
suit, on his way to an
INTERNATIONAL CULTURAL CONFERENCE (fare paid,
hotel arranged: now, Dogrose, you're

an established poet who gets asked to conferences.
Friend, go up higher:
Go to the top of the main staircase!)

Adriatic waves thump the hull. The big jets
scream like trapped gulls out on the tarmac.
Gales of the sea trapped permanently in metal.
Dogrose, neat-suited. Dramamined, a true
poet with his sea-water blood
pumping through valves of indolence and lust,
shy, watchful, quick to detect a slight,
haunted by rhythms of indifferent drums,
stung out of lethargy by images
which touch his flesh like loved fingers, he rises,
this poet, and obeys the metal speaker:

go to the top of the main staircase
go to the top of the main staircase

wave after wave of voyagers, outwardly
calm with discipline and information,
inwardly shrilling like electric bells

(who am I? what will become of me? WHERE
IS HOME? are they going to kill me?)

go to the top of the main staircase

the exact procedure of a slaughterhouse!
The herd, horns clicking, eyes rolling in fear,
bawling and fouling the neat passageway,
go to the top of the main staircase where
their necks are automatically, neatly, broken.

So Dogrose on his way to represent
poetry, the controlling agony, the creative
agony in the formal garden, goes
with the herd, to the top of the main staircase.

Relegatio. Technically the milder of the two Roman
forms of banishment. The other, *exsilium*, involved loss

of citizenship and confiscation of property, but at least
the *exsul* was free to wander the whole earth save within
a prescribed radius from the city of Rome. Tomis
(modern Kustenje) was obviously chosen as a place
Ovid would hate.

> *Relegatio* to Kustenje: the cold salt wind,
> treeless and marshbound, on a rocky coast,
> scene of an always-renewed humiliation:
> this was Ovid's luck.
> $\qquad\qquad\qquad$ And Dogrose's?
>
> oh, *exsilium*: he can go anywhere,
> blown along like a leaf, he can go anywhere,
> like a scrap of orange peel on the restless water,
> he can go anywhere,
> $\qquad\qquad\qquad$ except to the city.
>
> Dogrose, you long for the city,
> $\qquad\qquad\qquad\qquad$ the city of art,
>
> the ranged towers of fulfilment, the squares of
> $\qquad$ thought,
> the city where all cool poetry is true,
> where morning haze melts and everything is seen,
> but not wearily, not with hot sanded eyes,
> because everything is seen to be in motion,
> the motion of a dance, a perpetual arrival:
> Dogrose, Dogrose, you have dreamed of this city,
> but never entered it or heard its murmur,
> except sometimes in sleep, or in your art,
> when your art happened to be honest and fortunate.
>
> So, Dogrose, your sentence is *exsilium*.
>
>
> Ovid at least knew the city he longed for:
> pacing the cobbles of Tomis, gazing out
> with fear and loathing at the frozen marshes,
> he could have drawn you, on the spot, a plan

of the city he loved, told you in detail
what everyone was doing at that moment.

stone,
golden stone
warmth-retaining golden stone
sun-quickened warmth-retaining golden stone
noon-polished sun-quickened warmth-retaining
    golden stone

stairs
cool stairs
seen-through-doorways cool stairs
eye-resting seen-through-doorways cool stairs
impudent eye-resting seen-through-doorways cool
    stairs

girl
shadowy girl
warmth-retaining shadowy girl
impudent warmth-retaining shadowy girl
seen-through-doorway warmth-retaining shadowy
    girl

on the sensual stairs
                noon-polished

bright as the coins that buy her
clinking in my palm

after the wine and the good talk
the hearing of verses.

Yes, I remember the city
and the city's joys
and its golden stones

and I look out across these stiff salt grasses

Relegatio from the known, identified place:
or *exsilium* in a world of aching gaps,

94

of spaces where possibility might be, where
voyaging hope might find anything or nothing:

take your choice, and in either case,
and even if you have no choice at all,
go to the top of the main staircase!

    Now the deep Danube
is damned. Winter in the locked heart
of the poet, snow on the salt marshes:
millions of flakes falling on the endless Atlantic,
and on that other Atlantic of grass,
cruised by mammal ships.

        To the west
of the western landfall. Men know it only
by report. The grass
goes on for ever, and the dark-humped herds
no one can count.

        Ice tinkles in their coats
now, the same ice that rimes the heart of Ovid.
(Whither, unto the bed's foot, life is shrunk)
The Northern hemisphere endures, endures.
The red man makes a fire of buffalo dung
on the treeless plain (Lee Lubbers, are you there?
The Redskin also has his treasure amid
the unregarded, the carelessly dropped waste).

The great herds move. And with them move the
  men,
the women, and the children, and the tents.

    But progress came
    the iron ships came
    the railroads came
    the automatic rifle with
    telescopic sights, came

    If innocence exists
    we see it in that eye

that patient, shaggy head
but innocence is air
through which the bullet flies
through which the axe-blade falls

As it fell on the Jews
as it fell on the gipsies
innocent, the children
bewildered as bison calves
herded into the camps:

Django, pluck your strings
for the gipsies who were gassed
and the gipsies now in England
herded from their camps
legislated into despair
in England now: pluck, pluck
the taut strings of our hearts.

And Bill
will listen a while, and lift
his belled horn to his lips.
The buffalo went
the Indian went
(to zoos, in either case,
when they happened to survive)

Well, now it is all over
and the plains have dwindled
to a geographical expression
a certain colour on the map, no more,

I go sometimes to the zoo
to question the buffalo
who never replies

I bend over the railings
as he stands in his pen:
colossal head and round
dark eye remembering what?

Look at a buffalo's eyes
some time. Wide-set, reflecting, round,
the boss of a polished shield

But nothing shielded him.

Francis Parkman in *The Oregon Trail* (1847) describes
the life at Fort Laramie, at that time a trading station
entirely administered by the American Fur Company,
the nearest outposts of the United States Army being
seven hundred miles to the east.

The permanent inhabitants of the fort were Indian
employees, with a few white supervisors, but it was the
rallying-point for Indian tribes on the surrounding
plains and a stopping-place for every party of emigrants
on their way to Oregon and California. The Dakota
Indians, who at that time still felt themselves stronger
than the whites, would get wind of the arrival of a
wagon-train of emigrants at Fort Laramie, and a whole
village would present themselves and demand a 'feast' –
a cup of coffee and two or three biscuits. Parkman gives
an eye-witness account of the arrival of 'Smoke's
village' at the same time as that of a wagon-train, and of
how Smoke and his people set up their tents on the plain
behind the fort, so that a whole Indian village, loud with
dogs and children, was suddenly there as if it had arisen
from the bare earth.

'One evening about sunset the village was deserted.
We met old men, warriors, squaws, and children in gay
attire, trooping off to the encampment with faces of
anticipation; and, arriving here, they seated themselves
in a semicircle. Smoke occupied the centre, with his
warriors on either hand; the young men and boys came
next, and the squaws and children formed the horns of
the crescent. The biscuits and coffee were promptly
despatched, the emigrants staring open-mouthed at
their savage guests.'

Ovid got to Kustenje in the summer.
The cobbles sweated. The salt wind
scrubbed the squares with dry heat.
What kind of place is this?
                              Salt marshes,
rocks. Above, Odessa: below, Istanbul,
behind, Bucharest. Half-breed Greeks,
full-blooded barbarians. Shy eyes watching:
'This is the wicked poet sent from Rome,
to live here as a penance.'
                              'A penance? Here?
He'll soon get used to it, if he's a man.'

Unnerved. A few questions. Is this my house?
Are there any books in Latin? Does anyone
speak it, I mean correctly, like a Roman?
Do I sleep on this? Where is my servant?

A fat woman, broad-cheeked, her face secret,
speaking Samatian only.
                              She wipes her hands
ceaselessly on a coarse apron. Her husband
sweeps the courtyard. New shutters will be needed
against the winter.
                              The winter? When will that
        be?
Not long now. The Danube freezes
for three months. That's when they come.

When who come?
                              That's when they come,
in the winter.
                              They come,
                                          they come,
galloping, bows bent.
                              WHO COME?

98

Who? What does it matter who?
The ones who always come, to any outpost:
the pitiless fierce riders from out there.

Watch that weather, stranger. When you wake
to find the water in your pitcher frozen,
then one day, soon, you'll hear the drumming
    hoofs.

That's why we talk so much about the weather.
And why I, too, think of the weather in 1900.
That boy's starved feet cat-quick on the hot bricks.

Burning arrows in the thatch? He makes a home
here?
His hunger makes a home.

Yes, and those streets
in 1900, a boy of six years
walking those streets, thin, his clothes
of the cheapest, nearly worn out
before he got them: but hot
incitingly hot, under his feet, the brick
pavement, for some reason I always imagine
him in summer, narrow feet
on the hot bricks.
                    Polluted water
and a towpath with rank
nettles and grass: the thin boy
prowls amid jagged tins. Heat
glares from the blue sky. For some
reason I see him under that hard
blue sky always, smelling polluted
water, watching the smoke
trail its thick arms across, black on blue,
and the bricks hot.
                    Ah, because
it is my own childhood gives me
my vision of his, the streets were the same

after three decades, the same bricks
held the same heat:
                    I wandered,
more often in summer than winter,
smelt the canal, was hungry like him,
I mean like him in his inner hunger, I longed
to reach out, to live, beyond these hot
bricks and round black kilns. Home!
I never doubted it, my home was hunger,
that hunger my blood had caught
from his hasty blood.
                    I see 1900,
trouble in South Africa, volunteers
marching with silver bands down London Road:
I see the thin boy
hungry
always hungry
for food, for life, for the promise that rises
to his narrow feet from the hot bricks.
Where does the canal go? Who reads the signal
poured across the sky by the fat kilns?
Power, money, and trouble:
Wedgwood and Kruger, Spode
and Smuts.
            The old queen
turns in her bed and dies. The thin boy,
my father, sees his mother draw the blinds.

The blinds of home. The bailiff has the chairs.
The old queen dies. Grandmother draws the blinds
on the bare dusty room. End of a world.
The kilns go belching on, and Wedgwood is
A liberal M.P.
            The boy is hungry:
He needs so many kinds of nourishment.
His hunger came to me. I have it still.

Home, home! The narrow houses and the kilns,

The stinking water. The tip above the roofs.
And half a dozen brick town halls.

Why is it always summer in my dream?

Because of the hot sunlight in his eyes?

To speak of exile is to speak of home.
The drumming hoofs across the ice: the poet
listless, far from Rome. Seventy years ago
the smell of the canal and the fat kilns.
The burning arrows crackle in the thatch.
The lost plank floats in the scum-laden water.
The poet shivers. The thin boy dreams of life.

And we speak of home? Of leaving, and returning?
A shake of the dice-box. A cube of time
rolls.

       Ovid in Smoke's village. The feathered men
stare at the poet who wrote of one girl
turned to a river, another holding up
arms suddenly twigs and leaves. The plank
in the crushed weeds, inert in that canal,
reared up, hardened to stone, became a dolmen.

Dogrose, *miglior fabbro*, do up your belt:
the muzak ceases and the engines scream.
Back in the airport you were nowhere. Now
on the tarmac, soon at twelve thousand feet,
then at another airport, a bus, an hotel room,
the table and ashtrays of the conference,
still nowhere, always nowhere, and you ask
so piteously, *What am I to do?*

Why, Dogrose, plant a grove of cardboard trees
and walk beneath them in a nylon toga!
the raised plank is
dolmen and totem. Feathered men
file swiftly along the nettled towpath.

Smoke's village pitches camp at Stoke-on-Trent,
smoke's other village.

                             Dogrose, you seek a theme?

Still want to think and feel yourself a poet?
The dice of time is shaken, rolls and stops.
The Indians and the buffaloes are gone.
Kustenje has no poets, only Agitprop.
Pasternak appealed to Khrushchev against exile:
his Art of Love was more profound than Ovid's.
After his death, they jailed the one he loved.
The quick thin feet of that boy six years old
have passed across the stones, my friends:
have passed, and will pass, and are passing now.
And Dogrose climbs the international sky.

Green Fingers

to Elizabeth Jennings
in Oxford

The intricate city suspended above fire.
A pavement of logic strung on cables of faith.
Belief in the known fire and the unknown fire.
A programme for eternity rooted in time.
Expectations built stone by stone, like the square
towers seen from the river bank. Cool water,
cool stone. And underneath, the fire.

And the fire also is an intricate city.
Cat-walks of the damned, threaded with souls
all humping loads of disappointment. Fire
maddens their veins. Without punishment
would not the city pavements crack and vanish?

Perhaps these fictions are worth it, for the city.
The squared stones of faith, balanced above fire,
are solid under the wind-beaten towers:
and the towers point calmly towards the fiction of
        heaven.

System, system: that chiming Italian metre,
a threefold music for a threefold theme:
no hope: all hope: effortless fulfilment.

The abstract city of Dante holds also real
fountains that leap in the hot squares of Rome,
the Lambretta's cough in rainy Florence, its walls
flower-hung, picture-hung, throned in Tuscan
        pride –
no place on earth so solid and so fine.
I know your thought, Elizabeth: you long
to orchestrate a Tuscany of the mind:
as solid and green as those tower-crowned hills,
as native to the green as those white oxen.
                                    Squares,

a pattern of rectangles, a true city
where feet can wander and always find their way:
cafés where lovers or disputants can linger:

you write these things in your book of life, as I do.

Black tarantulas sidle along the cables of faith, which
have become threads of their rubbery bird-murdering
webs.

The warm spring mud is full of horse-leeches.

The Pope is a mandril. The Cardinals are mandrils. The
Archbishop's robe hides a narrow, haired baboon-body.
The floor of the confessional box is slippery with fruit-
rinds and stale droppings. All the time the saints absent-
mindedly scratch their rainbow-coloured tumescent
nates.

The pavement shivers. Leviathan is trying to batter his
way up from the underground lake.

The upper slopes of the Himalayas seem domestic and
companionable when viewed from the electrically-
cooled vacuum of modern loneliness.

The beautifully-swept boulevards go round in concen-
tric circles. You could walk and walk for your whole
life on bare clean asphalt, completely unmarked save
for, every few yards, a drop or two of spittle: the drool
of the police-dogs. You never see the dogs: they are
always round the next curve, and the next curve is
always the same as the one behind. Realizing that
walking will take you nowhere, you realize also that if
you stop walking you will instantly drop through a hole
in the pavement and hang on the spider-webs, twitching
and waiting.

Suddenly, to your joy and astonishment, the high con-
crete walls part to reveal a narrow path. You follow it
between board fences. A street, an ordinary human

street, with children marking out the pavement for hop-
scotch and a man oiling a bicycle! Are you home at last?
In the end house, faces appear at the window; hands
beckon. The door opens. Your room is ready. You feel
relief and gratitude; but, silently, they point to the cellar
steps descending steeply into the darkness.

Down *there?*

The cellar stairs are dark. I hear your tread.
Your fingers trace the cold and sweating wall.
The cellar is a household of the dead.

You never wanted to go down at all:
Whole weeks, whole months, you breathe that
    airless chill!
The stairs are broken. Now and then you fall,

Lie silent, then get up. Whose is the will
That pushes you inside and locks the door?
Or is it mindless? Does the abandoned mill

That swings its arms in the cold wind, know
    more
Than I what force it is that sends you down?
I fumble with the bolts. They will not draw.

You must stay there, queen of that fungus town
Throned amid nightmares, till the Thing relents,
Opens the door, and with a wondering frown

You climb, and find us here. Between descents,
You live like us: books, walks, the telephone:
All that long patience Oxford represents.

But down there, in a silence hard as bone,
Breathing through those interminable hours,
Sealed from our air and sunshine, cold, alone,

Somehow your magic works. Darkness devours
All love, all laughter drowns in the black slime:

and yet, from that dead floor, you raise up flowers.

When, patiently, up the dark stairs you climb,
Blinking a little in the sharpened day,
You never fail to tell us, *All that time*

In that dark place, I tended these: rich, gay,
Abundant, there they shine: you hold them out
As modestly as tea-things on a tray.

Green-fingered artist, I see you never doubt
Even in those lost days, denying, stark,
What is the work that you must be about:

A world of colour blossoming in the dark!
Hidden from anguish and the body's fears
Like trustful cattle in the wallowing ark,

Its seeds couch in a soil kept moist for years:
They grow towards your memory of the sun:
There must be something potent in those tears

With which you water them, for all that's done
And seen, and thought of, leaves its residue:
Art finishes what action has begun,

But only if its metaphors are true.
I see your colours and I catch my breath,
For joy that once again you have come through.

Your art will save your life, Elizabeth.

Music on the Water

to Bill Coleman
in Paris

and like
the river's slow insistence.

In winter, a great padlock. Tugs and strings of
    barges
fist-gripped. Summer, a cool flowing.
The sun hatches the shy turtle's eggs.

Sound moves across water:
axe-chop, bow-twang: did the Indians
sing? Or was silence their music?

The river orchestrates silence. It pours.
They looked at it and they said: *Mississippi*.

So time passed, without punctuation.
The river poured and grass waved
in the dateless wind. Red-skinned, high-cheekboned
    Adam
named the animals: *opossum, chipmunk*.

And sound reached out across water.

But out at sea, the corpses smacked down
into the waves, unweighted. White bodies were
    cheap:
still, a white sailor who died, at least
got cannon-shot at feet and head.
Sick, terrified black bodies
only just worth the cost of carrying
were chucked out if found to be dead
(putrid, not understanding, sick for Africa)
chucked out, like peelings from the galley
to float on the surface till the sharks came up.

Out at sea, the slave ships were coming.
Sound reached out across water:
dead-smack of corpse, gull-scream,

chop of the settler's axe, gun-crack and
whip-crack: in the steamy fields
the black backs bend, the long dark song goes up:
the American earth, no longer Eden:
and sound moves out across water.

Africa forgotten,
the hunter's green and yellow beads forgotten,
the snapping apart of the full bean-pod,
the stew simmered with thick yam-flour, forgotten.
The elephant's praisename is Laaye, signifying
'O death, please stop following me':
they forgot the elephant's village-shaking tread
but death did not stop following them.

Voodoo forgotten,
the necklace of teeth forgotten
and the witch-women in coastal areas
with skirts made from octopus tentacles
forgotten also

but the tentacles of misery, the tread
of death broad as the foot of Laaye:
these, they had no occasion to forget.

The Indians were gone
taking with them their music of silence:
now the black backs bent low, and the long dark
        song
moved out across the water:

sound of steamboat, of hammer and saw,
of locomotives, of clopping horses
and of the song of sorrowful memory,
the sound of unknown Africa.

And the cobbles of Europe
were already old:
                        the steep roofs
had kept out many seasons already
the iron cooking-pots of humble men
fed life, humble and recurrent life

stirred by women who bent and dreamed
lay down, rose up and dreamed:

down the slow lanes
the painted wheels were turning, dark-eyed women
crooning old foreign words to their shawled babies

words already old, the language of somewhere
forgotten,
the creak of axles, their home the roadsides of
Europe:

En mon pais suis en terre loingtaine

never at home, therefore always at home,
contained,

unspillable:
these were Django's people.
What centuries unwound,
what wars, what exiles, what thunder of surf,
cry of the new-born to the creak of axles,
what bruising of continent against continent,
before the two homeless songs made this their
home:
the plucked string and the quivering mettlesome
cry,
the two long journeys meeting here at last.

and Paris in the spring, the cold-eyed spring
hard buds, hard stones
Paris
the cold inexhaustible mother
feeding desire with hard nipples

spring:

time of the dispossessed, the voyagers,
envious only of solitude.

Sweet mother who leaves us all stranded
sweet mother who fuels our veins with hate

under whose bridges we crawl

in the rainy night
amorous as sparrows

the dark flowing Seine
inundating our nerve-centres

And Bill this is your second river
channel of paradoxes
ancient passageway of opposites.

Le sein is a masculine word:
a woman's breasts, masculine! what a race!
crazy inverted logic everywhere!
le sein is masculine, this is *la seine*,
the drag-net, the bulging tow, the trawl
that disdains nothing, the swag-belly,
full of mussels and contraceptives,
avid of mud, cress and semen,
la Seine, magnet of weightless suicides,
despair of anglers.

The first day, too inert to look for work, I borrowed a
rod and went fishing in the Seine, baiting with blue-
bottles. I hoped to catch enough for a meal, but of
course I did not. The Seine is full of dace, but they grew
cunning during the siege of Paris, and none of them has
been caught since, except in nets.
   – George Orwell, *Down and Out in Paris and London.*

A different river, Bill. But the same need.
Something human to make the cold ripples dance.
Something human out of the bell of your horn.

Aching Paris
those spring evenings in big ugly cafés
staring through plate glass at the clicking street
still unaccountably light at eight o'clock
millions of cigarettes fuming like rockets
the girls with alarm clocks ticking between their
      legs
the pavement sprouting dreams of Martinique

aching Paris, never resting
inexhaustible mother and ticking meretrix
timed so as to wake us in mid-orgasm
old twisted Paris, gaunt zoo of the poor,
circus ring where the sawdust is milled bone:

Et nous, les os, devenons cendre et pouldre.
De nostre mal personne ne s'en rie;
Mais priez Dieu que tous nous veuille absouldre!

Bill, it is you and only you she needs.
lip those notes! press down those cunning valves!

A thousand years have cropped that sated womb.
Ten centuries of eyesight have blanched the air.
Feet have scrubbed the stones down to dead rubble.

Even the Seine catches nothing but old string.
The European impulse has dried up.
Every seventy years a new lyricism:

She was miraculous! yes, yes, we admit it!
But now, the song-bag is finally sighed out:
different trade-winds are blowing.

Old icy cobbled Paris, twisted streets,
fifteenth century, before the slavers got going,
surf booming innocently on the African beaches
and the university of Paris already two hundred
       years old:
one of its graduates, bleeding from the face,
well known in that precinct, François Villon,
stumbles into the barber's shop, dropping blood.
'Friend, patch me up, I'm leaving.' 'Fighting again?'
His lip is gashed wide open. 'An insolent priest.
I sent him to the other world.'
The barber whistles, dabbing at the wound:
'That'll mean trouble with the authorities.'

François de Montcorbier, *alias* des Loges, *alias*
       Villon,
(En mon pais suis en terre loingtaine)

111

never from that time a stranger to trouble,
his neck never far from the hempen knot.

Freres humains qui apres nous vivez.
N'ayez les cuers contre nous endurcis

O death, please stop following me

Car, se pitie de nous povres avez,
Dieu en aura plus tost de vous mercis

O death, please stop following me
O death, please stop following me

And each continent sang its pure music.

Villon, fugitive, cudgelled, his bones cold,
laughing and singing his crystalline despair,
uttered the pure music of Europe

Je meurs de seuf aupres de la fontaine,
Chault comme feu, et tremble dent a dent;
En mon pais suis en terre loingtaine;

and under a copper sun
the pure music of Africa rose up:

flight of the egret in words:
repose of the bright parrot among leaves,
lidded pots of clay, woven shields,
quick strut of a disappearing bushfowl:
these things in words:
                    song, drum and chorus.

The bright feathers fade from the mind,
the hunter's mask, the dance,
feast after hunting, contentment among straw huts,
these fade from the mind:
images pasted over with fear,
fear of the whip, fear of the chain,
of the waves, of the sea-monsters,
of the tossing prison reeking with death:
then forgotten below this, the images,
buried in marrow and blood.

And they also journeyed
the black-eyed people from the forgotten country
painted Romany wheels strained through Europe's
    mud

from threat to threat
cursed, harried, their caravans
fired by the soldiery, and the villages
full of hostile eyes at shutters.

From threat to threat they went,
his people, and your people.

And the long journey met at last in Paris:
met, and flowed into music.
Paris, 1935:
the neon lights shone bright
on the dark river
and the epaulettes shone bright
on the shoulders of Hitler's generals
as they bent over maps
their criss-cross sights already on Paris
they thirsted for her
the Rhine was mad to flow into the Seine
to die of joy in her grab-net
as a man wants to drive his teeth
into the white shoulders of a girl
those monocled men spread out maps
Paris, Paris, white shoulders'
and behind them, the ovens
already going up
Herrenvolk
must not be jostled in the world's avenues
so build the ovens
Joe Louis knocked out Schmelling
so build the ovens
and build a special one for him.

And in neon Paris, Django strummed
his plangent greeting-chords to life

and your horn was at your lips
and sound moved out, Bill, across the water:
flow, Seine, flow, Mississippi,
flow, strangling Rhine!

Et nous, les os, devenons cendre et pouldre

And I, in by-passed England, rain on the window,
spin your records and groove down the centuries
hearing the creak of axles and the crack of whips
the murmur of women to their shawled babies.

The deep lanes of Europe: the sharks rising
to the unchained corpses: the uncatchable carp
in the *rusée* Seine, knowing all men's tricks:
knowing men to their depths, in the agony
of unillusion, as the whores
know them in the tall, scented houses,
as slaves in their patience know them
unbuttoned, unmasked, yet hung about with
    dreams
like mad vines swaying in the tropic night
huge flowers that when we touch them turn to
    scabs.

Bill, my friend, courteous and smiling,
my tall unruffled uncle, at ease in restaurants,
king of the world of easy handshakes,
anchored to Swiss Lily like a bronze statue
on a marble plinth, you know all this:

you and the gipsy Django sang it all.

And now that he is dead, you sing it still.
The night stirs the dark vines, the enslaved eyes
stare on the naked face of pitiable huge Man,

and sound, always your sound, moves out across
    the water.

114

Ferns

for Anthony Conran
in Bangor

Yours is the steep house on the steep hill.
Below, the hospital. Above, the college.
The town clings to the land's short shoulders.

You chose this place to meet your need for contrast.
Everything here pirouettes with its opposite
in a dance whose music your inner ear
holds cupped.
　　　　　　　Those ancient hard heads,
the clustered mountains, some of earth's oldest
　　　rocks,
light green or purple, grass, stone or heather,
changing with the light that walks among the
　　　clouds,
above the heavy layers of the sea
(unalterably of its own way of thinking,
dismantling and building, eating and disgorging,
cold and sensual with its own salt
and its own secrets):
　　　　　　　two grandeurs
to orchestrate with the ordinariness of the streets,
the commonplaces of shop-front and semi,
the leaded panes in the boarding-house front porch.
Now *there*'s a challenge for a true artist,
such as God, or one of his poor worshippers!

In Caernarvonshire. Gull-scream and cloud-drift.
On this long shelf, 'the stone's
in the midst of all' most literally.
The thin soil lies a few inches deep
spreadeagled over rock, strained through by rain.
Everywhere, boulders and outcroppings
prod grey through green. In valleys near the sky
the abandoned quarries sigh to the deaf wind:
thousands of tons of slate beneath your hand,

level green tracks where little railways climbed,
and higher up, shale. Scree. The Elephant's
long corrugated trunk, his patient head.

Nothing can live here that does not love stone.

Water among the rocks. The dark
drip into a stone cup. Perfection,
the natural chiselled goblet. But of a chillness
inviting nothing from the onlooker.
The water hurries as if to escape a plague,
keeping its cold integrity. It runs
and leaps down the unsunned cleft. The mountain
          listens.
                    And the fern holds on,
rooted in any cranny, green and curling,
its form a patient embroidery, a scroll,
one of a set of variations on
a shape basically as simple as an egg
and full of possibilities as a hand:
it grows, it climbs, it unfolds,
not to be questioned, permanently there,
younger than nothing but the rocks and water.

Or in the town. The steps behind your house.
Handrail and blackened brick. The fern is there
sprouting from crevices, ignoring our
broken-winded voices as we drag
ourselves up to the road that leads to the college.

They clench and curl towards the rainy sky.
And out in your back yard, in grey stone troughs,
are some you tend:
                    you garner, name, and love.

They come to my aid, Tony, your green friends:
your house-mates in their troughs of mould outside
your kitchen window: yes, they help me.
They bring me calming thoughts: like hard brooms

they sweep the hot pavement of my life
cleansing its dry surface like a cool green wind.
This is because they speak to me of beginnings,
and of the time before the beginnings:
millions of years of water, stone, and cloud.

Oh, it helps, on the hot pavement,
so crowded with bumping bodies, so littered,
rank with the sweat of toil and the sweat of fear,
it helps to be guided by those stubborn tendrils,
those unambiguous wavings of semaphore
from the other end of the ravine of time:
it helps, amid the jostling of impulses,
the snatching for scraps of love and shreds of
    pleasure,
amid the suction of lips, the slop and wallow
of digestion, the throbbing mast of lust,
it steadies me to think of the beginnings,
and of the time before the beginnings,

WHEN

life had not yet arrived

the vapour rising upward from the hot ball of earth had
condensed into thick clouds which continually let fall
their rain, hissing on to bare rocks too hot for the hand
(but there were no hands) and then gathering into
steamy pools and then into lakes and then into the
planet-girdling oceans, but such oceans! so clean and
empty, thousands of miles of water without one speck
of seaweed, not the smallest jellyfish, no hungry,
exploring crumb of life, only the plashing and tumbling
of the water and the drifting of thick white cloud, and
the beat of rain on the rocks: no cry of voice, no
thought, no desire, except perhaps the desire of earth
itself, deep in those veins of fire, the longing to be
swarmed over, to be trampled, populated, used:

AND WHEN

fear had not yet arrived

because of course there must have been movement,
rattle and slide of loosened stone, even thunder of surf
there must have been: surely there were storms, wind
must have hastened from one point of the compass to
another (but there was no compass, nor mind to reckon
its degrees), wind must have shoved at the rocks, piled
up the waves: there were certainly volcanoes, sudden
unmannerly lava-belchings with smoke and fire, and
who doubts that there were tornadoes, twisting up
columns of water, sending the great pillars walking on-
ward with idle, swaying menace: idle because no one
feared being sucked up or smashed, there was no
drowning, no burying, no overwhelming, no shrieking
for pity, no rattling the last desperate breath into the
terrified lung: there was movement, there was collision,
there was destruction, but there was no fear:

AND WHEN

love, equally, had not yet arrived

there was nowhere on the earth one single cluster of
organized matter which perceived another cluster of
matter organized in what was basically the same way,
yet with certain all-important and delicious differences,
and sent flashing like an electric hare round the circuit of
its nervous impulses the message: Happiness would be
to own *that*.

And all this nothingness took place in secret!
The clouds made a thick white curtain, translucent
but concealing, to ward off the brooding sun.

It must have been like an enormous bathroom.
So clean, so void of event: it rests me
to think of it, Tony!

Tugged every way by life,
when there seems too damned much of everything,
and I have fears that I may not cease to be,
but live on through storm's cycle and epicycle,
through aeons of devouring and of being devoured,
I like to think of those millions of years of nothing.

Of course, sooner or later the action had to start.
God, or whatever, would never have allowed it
to hang back for always.
                              So the hot gases, or
        something,
acted on by something, perhaps the strong sunlight,
began to form these complicated patterns
of chemical reaction, or something:
and after a lot of nobody-quite-knows-what,
something happened that we do not understand,
but we see it has an affinity with ourselves
and we call it 'life'.
                      Yes, 'life' began, that grand
solemn fever of which all of us are dying,
and even God has forgotten how to cure!

The shoots you cherish curl upwards from the
        stone.
They embody every kind of patience,
including that of your poems. The green they show
is earth's basic livery. Unconcerned at weather
that would lash back more opportunist flowers,
they acknowledge no environment as master.

Their one colour is stronger than the hue of
        flowers.
Basically simple in structure, their patience
gives them the holy power to astonish: they show
intricate lace-patterns, raising from cracks in the
        stone
delicate opening fingers to caress the weather.

This is why you love them, undiscourageable
    master,

intent on your page of cool petal and stone,
assembling grain by grain in the dispersing weather
a soil firm enough for your unsentimental flowers:
enamelled, regal, giving to life their master
the strong homage of art, which cannot show
love except where love is. Their glowing patience

mellows the air of your steep house, that stone
ledge where you perch above your century's
    weather
still as a hawk, waiting for movement to show
far down among the trembling grass and flowers,
no less potent than that fierce bird to master
your fluttering hunger with the hunter's patience,

yet unlike him in what your gestures show.
Life, not death, signals from your high stone:
the wish to tend and nourish, not the impatience
to scatter blood amid the scent of flowers:
not the suddenness of the chill and troubled weather
but the slow stubborn love of the art you master.

Poet, guard your love. Feed your rooted patience.
Only such as you will have any good to show
for these blank, scurrying years. The time of the
    stone
is on us now, the life-denying weather
of dust-storm and mistral. Withstand it, master,
and may your dreams be garlands of cool flowers.

How this time's dead weather bruises our living
    patience.
Thank God, in this place of stone, one knot of
    flowers:
Amid the bawling freak-show one quiet master!

Take the wind, poem, in your pregnant sails.

Turn our head towards less shallow waters.
He whom we praise is a poet, not a plant.
And yet:
my mind comes back to Ovid and his changes.
Sitting in Eirian's cottage above the sea,
I have no copy of *Metamorphoses* here,
but your own sheaf of poems of that name
gives me the images I want:
                              the rain is 'the time
of crossed circles', a girl's sleep floats downstream
in the guise of drowned Ophelia, also a swan
arching its lute-neck.
                      Ovid would have relished
your poems for their strong juxtapositions:
painting the country of your feelings as
'the strange land humped like a weasel's back
where bedouin ride'.
                     Tony, you take your risks
and root yourself high up on the cliff-face.

It is his suddenness you learn from,
that Roman, strong-willed, in his graver years
his imagination no longer like a furry bunny
hopping amid tangles, diving to a burrow,
but like an unexpected kangaroo
as yet undreamt of, leaping the steady walls
of Rome. His not-yet-exiled eyes
saw shape as motion.
                     And all true poets have
seen with the eyes of Naso, when the weight
of the month grows lighter, and sharp moon
grins down: then their tides pull like a woman's,
and Ovid's liquefaction flows to theirs.
'Daphne with her thighs in bark
Stretches towards me leafy hands':
This sight was vouched for in London, W.8:
the victor's leaf, the girl's blood yielding to sap

(much the same colour when enclosed in veins)!

So Ovid gives me the answer, in the end.
The hard spores of your art unfold to ferns:
the cool heraldic fronds, the ancient strength:
pain, love and knowledge rooted among the rocks.

And there is courage here, friend, for such as we,
making our music in a tone-deaf world.
The ferns grow green with or without approval.
They spread their fans whether they are seen or not.
There is much virtue in these ancient leaves.

From

Wildtrack

(1965)

Ars Poetica

Engrave the snowflake. But without hindering
   its downward
dance. Carve your biography in images,
one for each flake, and take as many
flakes as you need. But (this is your legendary
task) never hold one in your hand. The warm
touch of human skin melts them to water. (As
the man said, one's name cannot be written
there.) Engrave an image on each tumbling
weightless flake. Above, the opaque grey
future: underfoot, the trodden slush
of the past (dog-pee and fag-end speckle
an outline of geological dignity).
Only the falling snowflake is the Now.

To write of the Now on the down-drifting
frozen angel-feather of This, the revolving
snowflake in its carelessness of before
and after, to engrave particular facts,
specific adventures of eye and finger-tip,
and always with no break in the resigned
eager dance of the snowflakes, their sift and
   winnow:
this is your task:
                  BEGIN

   I think of January 1918
   the Germans breaking through on the Western
   Front BAM BAM WHEEEEE CRUMP and in
   Moscow and Petersburg snow falling
   and civil war BAM BAM. Snow
   seen by Alexander Blok
   lifted in spirals by the wind
   Alexander Blok watching the snow
   four January days. Engraving
   world history, the history of Russian
   heartbeats on unmelting

snowflakes despite BAM BAM. Crumple
of corpses soon to stiffen. Blok
graved with a diamond his nation's
heartbeats on twelve snowflakes.

Twelve snowflakes sifted down:
and a few more followed, partners
without volition. Only Blok
with one thin graving tool could image
January 1918 on twelve snowflakes
plus the odd few for luck.

I see that snow on the pavements
trampled into a paste with mud and spittle
I feel that wind
a man could lean against that wind
no overcoat
for the poor old woman who
looks up and reads
the banner strung between the houses

ALL POWER TO THE CONSTITUENT ASSEMBLY

Holy Mother of God she says

what a waste
all that cloth

And here come the Twelve
cracked boots and frayed rifle-slings
but their rifles in working order
ready for BAM BAM BAM

Twelve snowflakes caressed in midfall
by the cool fingertip
and the bright diamond
of Alexander Blok

Twelve snowflakes sifting down
and the odd few for luck

Vanya and Katya taking a sleigh-ride
Vanya the out-smarter
always with it Vanya
never misses a trick
and Katya
the officers' whore
with her stockings wedged full
of currency notes

Notes issued by the Kerensky government
yes that same Kerensky
who walked the other night
down the road near the house
where I John Wain sit writing this
in Oxford, England
Kerensky
himself a snowflake
still winnowing down
an old man with memories

Katya you officers' whore
you are wanted
wanted by the Twelve
a private has one too Katya
a worker, a man with empty pockets
has one too
it's time you tried it Katya
up to the neck you bitch

BAM BAM and the coachman
whips up his horses
Vanya gets away as usual
but Katya lies still

You bought it Katya
the Kerenkas in your stockings
paid for it

A snowflake Katya
                    trampled
                              underfoot

Twelve snowflakes sifting down
and the odd few for luck.

Then the bourgeois
O God yes the bourgeois
he stands on the corner with his fur
collar turned up and his mangy
bow-wow beside him

His collar is turned up so far
only the tip of his nose
sticks out

We needn't feel sorry for him
any more
a snowflake settles on the tip of his nose
a falling snowflake
lost
like Katya
yes we feel sorry for Katya
but not for the bourgeois on the corner
BAM BAM BAM
he sucked our blood long enough
and you dog scoot
scuttle away
                    you hear?

But he follows
tail down. Old Russia
is dead. Old Russian ways
are dead and here come
the Twelve leaning against the wind
stumping in the snow
one lags behind
thinking of Katya
a dead piece of free-market
luxury with a sweet birthmark
on her shoulder but never mind
the dog's tail is well down

Old Russia must die BAM
BAM

Alexander Blok with his face pressed to the pane
saw twelve snowflakes fall that can never fall again

Clumsy cracked boots stamped through the spiralling snow
the Twelve were marching the way they had to go

their history was already written, they had no choice
only the dog howled, only the old woman's voice

came to Alexander Blok's ear as he gazed down
from his unsleeping window and saw the town

the streets the markets the canals and the faces
upturned to the pitiless snowstorm that left no traces

of the beggar's spittle or the bourgeois' terrified eyes
or the Kerenkas wedged in the warmth of Katya's thighs

Speak to me tense poet from your visionary gloom
say why you leave your chair and pace about your room

confess Alexander Blok confess what you see
as the twelve march straight ahead singing softly

Confess that your eyes grow wide and your reason rambles
as you smell the hot blood from the human shambles

when the Twelve shall break open the vials of their wrath
and pity like that starved cur be kicked from their path

Confess Alexander Blok that you hear the screams
of children at night dragged from the warmth of their
      dreams

running to hide in alleys full of demented figures
running blindly as the Twelve press their steel triggers

You who see Jesus Christ at the head of the Twelve
is it the wounds of humanity he comes to salve

or is it not rather a new furnace he prepares
for the flesh that only in death lays down its cares

is it not rather the mighty embrace of death
he has ready for these creatures of blood and breath

Blok you foresee the hour that must come to birth
when you will cry 'the woodlouse has inherited the earth'

These will be the years of the mindless gnawing louse
when central and eastern Europe is one huge torture-house

when the Rhine and the Moskva flow between aching walls
and the sky is empty where the human victim calls

You Alexander Blok foresee this in your agony
and you are right to see Jesus Christ who cannot die

Leading the Twelve into those years of crucifixion
for Christ walks on earth only in one direction

it is always towards the blood-soaked Cross that he moves
to the sound of distant trumpets and approaching hooves

for Christ's way forward lies through the gates of pain
and he has come to be crucified again

with the children hiding in the alleys and the shivering
        brutes
who were men until the Twelve began to shoot

but when they heard the guns went down on hands and
        knees
and chewed bitter grass under the leafless trees

Confess confess Blok you see the children's eyes
as dry and empty as the unpitying skies

the cell doors will slam, the soldiers will strut like geese
Christ will be crucified by the secret police

and to see the white streak of hope beyond this night
is beyond the reach of your pale dilated sight

you will sink without hope into silence and neglect
and your world be left to the mad dog and the insect

your window will be blank above the windy square
when your eyes have closed with weariness and despair

and yet despair is not the end, Blok your voice will sound
when the Twelve you loved lie deep in the frozen ground

for you watched them move forward against the mocking
    wind
you saw the tattered cloth of revolt that they pinned

over their naked flesh in that freezing air
you saw their harsh humanity as they laughed and swore

and as you watched the Twelve marching with iron feet
you loved them, you longed for sheaves of golden wheat

ripe fruits and flowers to toss on the hard stone
that the Twelve might have something they could call their
    own

beyond the frown of vengeance and the doubled fist
and so you saw dimly in the freezing mist

the figure of Jesus Christ arisen from his sleep
leading the twelve like shepherds to the hungry sheep

this was your vision on the night of the black sky
and I honour you Alexander Blok with your dilated eye

you felt the hunger of those lost and homeless crowds
and your pity called down Christ from above the clouds:

I feel it too, mindless as the falling snow
that prints its ironic kiss on the white faces below

I see the faces upturned amid the unceasing snowflakes
and I see the poet who weeps and aches

seeing already the world of the woodlouse-state
in which the cry of the living man will come too late

longing to walk with the twelve, to share their load
yet fearing the eyeless walls which line that road

fearing the dead bricks and the soundproof air
where the footsteps of the Twelve echo only despair

confess Alexander Blok you fear those walls
between which the twelve go forward like doomed animals

and the figure of Christ dwindles to a scarf of mist
and becomes again the pale Christ whom Judas kissed!

Selves

a man walks out alone
his two feet sucking
like a fly's feet at the tilted earth
alone
save for the other within his skin
always that other
hidden from him, yet present
meaningful,
         qualifying,
                  expert in *nuance.*
In the broad shaft of the sun
the man alone throws a shadow

In the dark sea of sleep
someone beside him stirs the fine sand

fish dart questioningly
birds peer from the trees

always that other
stays close

Je est un autre!

The day-self moves in a broad shaft.
The night-self is secret and daft.

The day-self joins with eager others.
The night-self has no friends, only brothers.

The day-self is poltroon or hero.
The night-self is picaro, pierrot.

The day-self can choose to tell lies.
The night-self speaks truth, or he dies.

The Day-Self Contemplates
the Defeat of Time

In the rain-forest I found, the air is quiet.
Still pools collect at the feet of the great trunks:
moss grows in the green silence, creepers stir
in a breeze too faint for a girl's cheek to feel.
There, nothing dies.
                    What is discarded sinks
and pulses alluvial, feeding the deep roots.
Daylight is filtered here, and darkness lit
by phosphorescence. The presence of the forest
never sleeps, nor ever quite awakes.

To move in the forest I discard flesh.
Only the mind has passport here, for time
is cruel to the body, tolerating
only that shudder of loin on loin that brings
futurity in the endless line of births.

No flesh can walk in the forest. The still air
blows easily into the porous cells of thought
and only thought.   I moved among the trunks
and heavy stems, I heard the dripping leaves
conversing with the moss, and the thick stems
of rubbery marsh-plants eased to let me pass.

I went along the path that was no path
and the forest took me, silent, welcoming:
and as my vision opened in the gloom
of that green stillness, I saw others there.
Calm, solitary shapes resting among the leaves
or standing by the always-motionless trunks,
they disregarded me and each other.

                    What
had made them free of this primeval peace?
How had they left their flesh, that prey of time,
and come unhampered under these colonnades?

And then I saw that none was empty-handed.

Each held, like a prize too joyous to put down,
the thing that he had made. Only this magic
was strong enough to lull the wrath of time,
and bring each maker into his fulfilment, here,
under the inexhaustibly fertile boughs.

Who first coiled springs? Fashioned a stirrup, or
thought of a book which opened on a hinge?
Drew sounds from wood and string, or named a
        bird?
His liberated self was here.
                                        I trod
the unmapped forest, marvelling, and not
I only, but others among living men:
the thoughtful-eyed, those able for an hour
to turn from the highway of the Here and Now,
leaving the flesh to cool itself awhile,
and wander for their delight in the quiet shade,
meeting now this achievement, and now that:
all turbulent minds now quiet, all fulfilled
in joyous contemplation: how this one had
designed a palace, that one distilled a drug
that could heal pain, another found a sea,
a fourth made fables that enriched men's lives.

All marvelled, and I marvelled with the rest:
but none stayed long: the calm of the great forest
could not be borne by those whose flesh was warm
and cried its hungers and its urgencies,
calling them back with swift and bitter cries:
summoned, they hurried off, and others came,
but scampered in their turn: and I, like them,
feeling my respite at an end, bowed low
to those indifferent presences, and left.

Back in the world of time, I hungered, gasped
in the raw air of contingency, and gripped

what solace I could find, like all the rest.
But the rain-forest is with me in my dreams:
and at some moment of freedom, when I feel
the hot clasp of the body slacken, and
the steel handcuffs of necessity click apart,
I shall walk once again beneath those boughs,
and breathe the air of the place where nothing dies.

The Night-Self Contemplates
the Arrival of Consciousness

Rich blood disturbed my thought
I knew no shape nor size
I wondered, and was not:
Cradled in salt, I had
No tears to dim my eyes:
My coupled veins were glad.
Love held me cradled there:
But still I dreamed of air.

I fed on love alone
Yet in its tender rind
My brain cried out for bone.
Love held me soft and coiled
O but the mind, the mind!
That tenderness was foiled:
I writhed in my own heat:
I willed my heart to beat.

I shouldered love aside
the cold air spoke my name:
I clutched the air: I cried!
My mother's flesh lay spent,
Cool ashes after flame.
She sighed: she gave consent:
Caressed by light, I lay
Small in the human day.

Flow like milk,
stand like a table,

dance like fire,
bounce like a bed,
world of my wonderment!

milk flows over

tongue and throat,
whiteness is sweet:

table stands dark,
good to hold,
sharp to hit:

fire dances bright
and wicked!
BACK
back
to safety
mouse in hole!

bed holds cool,
dips, waves, is
comfort to the toes.

Next, out through the door. A rippling
voyage into the bigger air. The sky
isn't a ceiling! Cool flagstones, dirt,
miracles waiting.
                    Get down, feel it!

Spiders watch. A world under each leaf.
Dew soaks my feet. I scramble up rough
bark. Benediction of tree and wall:
my friends that waited for me!

Not only friends.
Protection ended back there.
This world is full of sharpness. A bird
sings, then twangs and chops a worm.
Toads get squashed. My heart knots,
hard as a stone with pity. Perplexed,
a beetle kicks on his back. Won't someone help
     him?

Not me.
I'm afraid.

Then
the change of gear, climbing whine and scream
of the machine running faster and wilder,
its driver helpless, eyeing the dials,
his hands in his swaying lap. Madness
stalks the arteries. The thrush sings
in a forgotten tongue. Who wished this trouble
    on me?

Difference, potent and sly, what is it they hide?
Look, it is something they carry close to
    themselves.
Their eyes tell of it. But in what language?
If only I dared ask them to let me look!

Tall
the garden is full of animals
herself among them
Katya with the Kerenkas next to her thighs
an animal like the rest
tall
unfevered
as I can never be.

Now my body is made,
Now I stand in my fulness,
the road climbs always uphill.

The Rib

Sonnet:
to Jeanne Duval

Honey and feathers, silk of the inside lip
thick breath, hot heart, blind trembling at the
    knees:
her lacing fronds, his urgent slide and grip:
the sensual symphony is scored for these,

and these you gave: more still: the subtle drums,
spilt coffee on a white and starchy cloth
(through pampas grass the svelte procession comes,
the cool delicious taper claims its moth).

Only those unseen wings within him flapped
wild to be soaring in unperfumed air.
They itched beneath his skin. He paced the room,

sick with that throbbing pain: but flew nowhere.
His naked shoulders never grew a plume.
It was his lust, not yours, that held him trapped.

Hold tight for a steep dive. Bolt your
stomach into place, Jack. An insanely
intrepid dive through the steep surprising
air. Then smack into (with a plume
of spray) the salt water of our beginnings.
The bitter water that gives life. The end
of all our dreams of coolness and purity.
But first, a climb. Our dive starts from the
spindly ladders of a cosmic farce.

The day God slipped Adam a Mickey Finn!

Did you ever hear tell of it?
Well, Genesis is built
round belly-laughs but this one
is a boffo. The burlesque houses
of all time echo with that roar

of helpless laughter. Grimaldi,
Little Tich, W. C. Fields, you are
made truly after the image of God. To squirt
water from your button-hole, squelch
a custard-pie right in that sober citizen's
well-shaven jowls, that's true
piety.
           No disrespect,
I like jokes myself. They help one to face
seriousness, by coming at it sidelong.
But this was *the most!* Think of it: he's
lonely, tells the Chief he needs a girl.
It's creepy in the evenings, with no one
to answer your voice, or tell you please
to make up the stove. Eden? It's no
great draw without someone along to talk to
about how nice it is.
           So the Chief
says, Yes, all right, and then
WHAM! slips him a knock-out drop. Imagine that!

Ay, thou poor ghost, we will imagine that.
That sleep of Adam's, that thick restless swoon,
that coma hung with shadows and sharp dreams,
snakes crawling down the walls, fat spiders in
the bath (look that one up in Freud, fellows),
eyes sealed by God's occluding touch, teeth
      clenched,
look how his hands open and shut – he wants
to fight the beasts that attack him in his dream!
Hear him keep moaning? Adam, I would not
wish such a sleep on you.
           But that's not all!
The act gets better! What a genius, this
cosmic comedian. Out of his bag
he takes a jemmy and a silken mask.
A choker round his throat, a greasy cap.

He's going in for burglary! Before our eyes
he opens up the straight man's side and takes
– you'd never guess it – one of his ribs. Yes, you
heard me! I thought I'd never stop laughing. The
theatre was shaking, even the usherettes
couldn't stop watching the show. Why, I'd
go crazy if I had to watch the act
again. It was *too much*.
                    He takes this rib –
now look, ask anybody, don't believe me –
and says to him (still lying there asleep)
'You asked for it,' he says, 'you poor bastard' (or
something like that) and getting out some tools
and welding equipment, right there before our eyes
he makes it into a WOMAN!
                    Well, you can
imagine how that brought the house down. I can
still hear the way they clapped and cheered. Well, I
    mean!
Conjuring on top of an act like that!
'Okay,' he says, 'it's all
over,' and the straight
man, Adam, gets up and takes a bow,
then all of a sudden he says 'Where's my
RIB!' and down comes his hand on that side – 'Hey!
Come back here! I'm a rib short!' Laugh? They
started again, till I thought they'd die. Honest!
I'll give him that, this Adam was quite
good in the part. I mean, he made it live.
'Where's that rib?' he says again, and 'Help!'
Just as if anybody could
help him! So of course everyone laughed
again. And *then* – just picture it! – he comes
slap face to face with this babe!

Well, after that the band just had to start
playing and the stage was cleared

for the performing seals.
                                    What else?
A trouper knows when an act reaches its
natural finish. No one could laugh any more. I
    found
tears on my face. That's how hard I'd been
either laughing, or something.
                                    Well, I *mean* . . .

Post-operational

His eyelids opened. Light hammered on his nerves.
The tall grass heaved, with fever or desire.
The garden rocked him with its gentle curves.

The loneliness that coiled its rusty wire
about his heart, had parted. He was free.
Love shimmered like the air above a fire.

This was the miracle that had to be.
Naked, confiding, near enough to touch,
motionless in the moving light stood she.

Was he not blest beyond analysis?
His body had no doubts: its good was here:
and, dolphin-jumping in those waves of bliss,

worshipped the moon that burned so hard and
    clear,
worshipped the tides that made the waters dance.
O gentle earth! O crystal atmosphere!

Yet there was fear within his avid glance.

*To me it was highly comick, to see the grave Philosopher – the Rambler, –
toying with a Highland beauty! – But what could he do? He must have been
surly, and weak too, had he not behaved as he did. He would have been
laughed at, and not more respected, though less loved.*

    Boswell, The Journal of a Tour to the Hebrides with Samuel
Johnson, LL.D., *1786.*

The Highland Girl contemplates Samuel Johnson

They sat me on his knee for a joke,
after dinner.
At first, I was afraid.

The fire was warm, and he sweated.
My body felt heavy as a pony's.

Torchlight danced on his forehead:
I wanted to touch his eyes,
They were the colour of longing.

The men raised their glasses, and laughed.
Everybody talked very loud.
I would not have been afraid to comfort him,
Had they been quiet.

He held my hand a moment, then let me go.
In the night, I woke,
roused by my own weeping.

Sonnet: Act IV, Scene iii

'Paint till a horse may mire upon your face!'
Mad Timon screamed to those two pleasure-girls,
Raving to drown them in his own disgrace:
What did they answer? Shrug, and toss their curls?

Furs, silks, fine hangings, asses' milk, and pearls
Lying in cups of wine: a scented place
Among the cushions: spasms and cunning twirls,
The stallion member upright as a mace –

Things without words! Talk was a stink of breath.
Bodies like theirs were made to drive men mad:
What would he have them do? Scrub kitchen floors?

Years later, dying amid rags and sores,
They thought of Timon's frenzy, and were glad:
His curses warmed their blood, that cooled towards
    death.

The Night-Self Sees All Women
in One Woman

From clay to sky
from the close-clasping
roots' tunnel to the free
fairway of starlight and openness
I trace your image,
Katya, one name for all women,
now crumpled dead on the snow
kissed to death by the cold bullets of the Twelve
and now shining moon-like full in their eyes
rising over the Twelve into the unbiddable sky
and now again sinking
settling into warmth, a nest,
close on the companionable earth:
always I trace you Katya
in many places
seeking and finding
wearing out place, time,
identity.

My need is close-knit,
earthworm-creeping, leech-lipping
and also wind-under-the-feathers
high-spiralling.

My need is fish, buffalo, piston:
and you are all. In the tall wheat
the mouse builds a swaying house:
long tails twine for love.
Thin fish dart, but an oyster swims
slower than a tree grows:
every grace, any place is
yours. Like printed eyes
that stare from torn paper on a hoarding
you hold my gaze. All
life is your holy mountain.

I see you now Katya

even so distant, I see you
against the black sky of threats and questions
my eyes hold you
not even a woman
not even a feminine shape
but a streak of light
red and glowing, cool and gleaming
light from a fire of comfort
or the hot coals of desire
or light from a beacon
the pale urgency of a flare
or light from the steady moon:
every kind of light has majesty
and authority, and you
have all, at all times
Katya
unknown woman of the night
of Alexander Blok
and of my clinging night

I see you there so clearly
a stripe of light
against the black
the signal of our longing, our suffering
the ecstasy of our fulfilment
and the promise of our human future
unquenchable

From

Weep Before God

(1961)

Laugh before men, weep before God
Jewish Proverb

The New Sun

The new sun rises in the year's elevation,
Over the low roof's perspective.

It reveals the roughness of winter skin
And the dinginess of winter clothes.

It draws, with a hard forefinger,
a line under the old ways.

Finis! the old ways have become obsolete,
The old skin, the old clothes.

This same sun, like a severe comet,
rises over old disappointments.

It makes us cry out in agony,
this peeling away of old sorrows.

When the sun foretells the death of an old sorrow,
the heart prophetically feels itself an orphan;

a little snivelling orphan, and the sun
its hard-hearted parish officer.

Dear gods, help us to bear the new sun!
Let our firm hearts pray to be orphaned!

Apology for Understatement

Forgive me that I pitch your praise too low.
Such reticence my reverence demands,
For silence falls with laying on of hands.

Forgive me that my words come thin and slow.
This could not be a time for eloquence,
For silence falls with healing of the sense.

We only utter what we lightly know.
And it is rather that my love knows me.
It is that your perfection set me free.

Verse is dressed up that has nowhere to go.
You took away my glibness with my fear.
Forgive me that I stand in silence here.

It is not words could pay you what I owe.

Poem Without a Main Verb

Watching oneself
being clever, being clever:
keeping the keen equipose between *always* and *never*;

delicately divining
(the gambler's sick art)
which of the strands must hold, and which may part;

playing off, playing off
with pointless cunning
the risk of remaining against the risk of running;

balancing, balancing
(alert and knowing)
the carelessly hidden with the carefully left showing;

endlessly, endlessly
finely elaborating
the filigree threads in the web and the bars in the
        grating;

at last minutely
and thoroughly lost
in the delta where profit fans into cost;

with superb navigation
afloat on that darkening, deepening sea,
helplessly, helplessly.

This Above All is Precious
and Remarkable

This above all is precious and remarkable,
How we put ourselves in one another's care,
How in spite of everything we trust each other.

Fishermen at whatever point they are dipping and lifting
On the dark green swell they partly think of as home
Hear the gale warnings that fly to them like gulls.

The scientists study the weather for love of studying it,
And not specially for love of the fishermen,
And the wireless engineers do the transmission for love of
   wireless,

But how it adds up is that when the terrible white malice
Of the waves high as cliffs is let loose to seek a victim,
The fishermen are somewhere else and so not drowned.

And why should this chain of miracles be easier to believe
Than that my darling should come to me as naturally
As she trusts a restaurant not to poison her?

They are simply examples of well-known types of miracle,
The two of them,
That can happen at any time of the day or night.

Anecdote of 2 a.m.

'Why was she lost?' my darling said aloud
With never a movement in her sleep. I lay
Awake and watched her breathe, remote and
    proud.

Her words reached out where I could never be.
She dreamed a world remote from all I was.
'Why was she lost?' She was not asking me.

I knew that there was nothing I could say.
She breathed and dreamed beyond our kisses'
    sphere.
My watchful night was her unconscious day.

I could not tell what dreams disturbed her heart.
She spoke, and never knew my tongue was tied.
I longed to bless her but she lay apart.

That was our last night, if I could have known.
But I remember still how in the dark
She dreamed her question and we lay alone.

Distances To Go

Yes, when you die, so much depends
on how long a journey it involves
as particle to particle descends.

I've known people prefer, like wolves,
to lope with bellies almost touching the earth
(it makes them feel insecure, the way it revolves).

And too high fliers disintegrate, falling. It's not worth
bothering where their grains meet the ground,
they seem to be saying; as if air, not mud, gave birth

to their rare natures. Some, by contrast, are found
hanging in attics or otherwise not caring why,
how, or through what arc of sky they were downed.

The ones I like best come spiralling from high
up, all right, but in no wise blurringly far from
the tussocky staid earth where, calmly, they look to
lie.

Anniversary

These are my thoughts on realizing
That I am the same age as my father was
On the day I was born.

As a little scarlet howling mammal,
Crumpled and unformed, I depended entirely on
    someone
Not very different from what I am today.

When I think this over,
I feel more crumpled and unformed than ever:
I ask myself what I have done to compare with *that*.

It also makes me aware, inescapably,
Of having entered upon the high table-land,
The broad flat life of a mature man.

Where everything is seen from its actual distance,
E.g. childhood not so remote as to seem a boring
    myth,
Nor senility as something that awaits other people.

But deeper than that,
It is like entering a dark cone,
The shadow thrown across my life by the life it derives
    from.

And deeper than that still,
It is the knowledge that life is the one communicable
    thing.
It called. I heard it from where I slept in seed and
    liquid.

The patterns of seed and brine coalesced in a solemn
    dance,
Whence my life arose in the form of a crest,
And has carried itself blindly forward until now.

In ignorance of its uniqueness until now,
Until I stumbled over these thoughts solid as bricks.
And like bricks fearsome in their everyday squareness.

To Be Continued

It was a world without women,
They stalked across, the heroes of our boyhood,
Their shoulders forming the giant shape of
    courage.
They fought big cats or skidded round banking,
Buried their blades behind the heads of sharks,
Cried to the crocodiles, 'Here comes a man!'
    then dived.
Through vistas of serials they strode,
Bravely enduring the tattooist's needle,
Taking from foreigners no back-chat:
Fisting through palisades of wops and japs,
Trusting no dago,
Except the crack-shot gaucho.

By the green hedges we hid in their summer
    shadows.
Their lives were geared to the single shaft of
    courage:
Our tired fathers, brief-case and Morris,
Were men in a different manner.
We sniffed at the mild fields in their simple
    drizzle:
No cactus towered in the garden.
Turning the pages, absorbing our patchwork
    legend,
We bided our time for adventure:
All we needed was inches.

But all the time we were reading,
Our epic world was slowly listing over:
Time sprang a leak and our immunity
Sighed out like gas before we noticed.
Yes, hanging rapt above the dog-eared page
Chewing on dreams of manhood, simmered
    tender
On formula's gas-ring,

We never raised our eyes to see
The anaconda inching down the trunk,
The cruel Redskin aiming.

At last the Chinese pirates of desire
Rushed in a body: with the captain shot
Dead in the wheel-house, the chart of boyhood
    lost,
Our gallant tramp hove to:
At the swing of a linen skirt we struck our
    colours.

This was the real jungle of claw and creeper.
Macaws flashed in the green light, but we knew
No language of signals: tenderfeet all,
We roamed for escape as far as Klondyke and
    Yukon.
The Mounties always get their man. We were
So lately the Mounties: suddenly, now, the men.

So we abandoned ship, camped on an ice-floe.
Shouting 'mush' we started the long trek:
The walruses bobbed on the water in mockery.
It was all over, and we knew it.
Our tents whisked away in the fifteenth-year
    blizzard.

Sadly we packed away our heroes.
Goodbye to the stern-jawed men of decision!
Their adventures were too tame,
They who had never bitten the wormy apple.

Now we stood alone facing the mad horns,
Knowing neither flight nor courage would save
    us,
Neither truth nor lies;
We must go down where sharks wheeled in the
    gloom,
Do battle with the unfair octopus:

For the press-gang of lust and heartbreak were
    on us,
And pleasure winked like the deluding sea.

Perhaps, one day,
When the years have rolled in a ragged circle
To where the eggs of motive lie in their nest,
We shall go back to our heroes.
The legionaries will stand for the last parade,
Minor characters dead of cafard and thirst,
Who strained after a mirage of eyelashes,
And the cold bugle will sound.
The survivors will get their passage home,
There, by firelight, to re-enter the land
Of the cool freeman whose silhouette conceals
No awkward bag of honey; be once more
Like him, exempt from the swollen itch of
    liking,
And only in dreams
Remember the thicket and the misleading
    passage.

To a Friend in Trouble

On those sharp edges of your broken love
You cut your veins, which do not leak out blood,
But suck in trouble, trouble, to your heart:
What can I say? except that all about us
I see a time of melting, a time of unloosing;
And on my own life's flat horizon, also,
The clouds swim up.
So many faiths dry up or slide away,
So many lovers I see with averted faces
Who wander, and will not stay to be pacified.
Now all our hearts, I think,
Suck in this scalding drug through broken veins,
This dry, ammoniac, destructive pain.
I do not know what I should say to you:
It is the madness of summer beats us down,
The red-eyed sunshine and the pelting rain.
I stand beside you empty of all comfort,
Except to say that now your love is smashed
And gashes at your veins, I feel your pain:
And in these throbbing nights I also see
Those broken edges in my doubtful dreams.

Brooklyn Heights

This is the gay cliff of the nineteenth century,
Drenched in the hopeful ozone of a new day.

Erect and brown, like retired sea-captains,
The houses gaze vigorously at the ocean.

With the hospitable eyes of retired captains
They preside over the meeting of sea and river.

On Sunday mornings the citizens revisit their beginnings.
Whole families walk in the fresh air of the past.

Their children tricycle down the nineteenth century:
America comes smiling towards them like a neighbour.

While the past on three wheels unrolls beneath them,
They hammer in the blazing forge of the future.

Brooklyn Bridge flies through the air on feathers.
The children do not know the weight of its girders.

It is the citizens carry the bridge on their shoulders:
Its overhead lights crackle in their blood vessels.

But now it is Sunday morning, and a sky swept clean.
The citizens put down the bridge and stroll at ease.

They jingle the hopeful change in their pockets.
They forget the tripping dance of the profit motive.

The big ships glide in under the high statue,
The towers cluster like spear-grass on the famous island.

And the citizens dream themselves back in a sparkle of
     morning.
They ride with their children under a sky swept clean.

Dream on, citizens! Dream the true America, the healer,
Drawing the hot blood from throbbing Europe!

Dream the dark-eyed immigrants from the narrow cities:
Dream the iron steamers loaded with prayers and bundles:

Breathe the ozone older than the name of commerce:
Be the citizens of the true survival!

A Handshake for
Brave Culture-Uncles

As mice tread round in drums for exercise
Or cage-birds walk up ladders to ring bells,

So you, good hominids, mime Tarzan bold,
Swinging on nylon ropes from tree to tree.

'Big game stampede to safety when we scold!
At every smirk a reputation dies!'

So: thump your chests, and roar. Then home to tea.
How like a window-box this jungle smells!

Au Jardin des Plantes

The gorilla lay on his back,
One hand cupped under his head,
Like a man.

Like a labouring man tired with work,
A strong man with his strength burnt away
In the toil of earning a living.

Only of course he was not tired out with work,
Merely with boredom; his terrible strength
All burnt away by prodigal idleness.

A thousand days, and then a thousand days,
Idleness licked away his beautiful strength,
He having no need to earn a living.

It was all laid on, free of charge.
We maintained him, not for doing anything,
But for being what he was.

And so that Sunday morning he lay on his back,
Like a man, like a worn-out man,
One hand cupped under his terrible hard head.

Like a man, like a man,
One of those we maintain, not for doing
        anything,
But for being what they are.

A thousand days, and then a thousand days,
With everything laid on, free of charge,
They cup their heads in prodigal idleness.

A Song about Major Eatherly

The book (Fernard Gigon's Formula for Death – The Atom Bombs and After) also describes how Major Claude R. Eatherly, pilot of the aircraft which carried the second bomb to Nagasaki, later started having nightmares. His wife is quoted as saying: 'He often jumps up in the middle of the night and screams out in an inhuman voice which makes me feel ill: "Release it, release it".'
Major Eatherly began to suffer brief periods of madness, says Gigon. The doctors diagnosed extreme nervous depression, and Eatherly was awarded a pension of 237 dollars a month.
This he appears to have regarded 'as a premium for murder, as a payment for what had been done to the two Japanese cities'. He never touched the money, and took to petty thievery, for which he was committed to Fort Worth prison.

Report in The Observer, August 1958.

I

Good news. It seems he loved them after all.
His orders were to fry their bones to ash.
He carried up the bomb and let it fall.
And then his orders were to take the cash,

A hero's pension. But he let it lie.
It was in vain to ask him for the cause.
Simply that if he touched it he would die.
He fought his own, and not his country's wars.

His orders told him he was not a man:
An instrument, fine-tempered, clear of stain,
All fears and passions closed up like a fan:
No more volition than his aeroplane.

But now he fought to win his manhood back.
Steep from the sunset of his pain he flew
Against the darkness in that last attack.
It was for love he fought, to make that true.

II

To take life is always to die a little: to stop
any feeling and moving contrivance, however ugly,

unnecessary, or hateful, is to reduce by so much the total
of life there is. And that is to die a little.

To take the life of an enemy is to help him,
a little, towards destroying your own. Indeed, that is
    why
we hate our enemies: because they force us to kill them.
A murderer hides the dead man in the ground:
but his crime rears up and topples on to the living,
for it is they who now must hunt the murderer,
murder him, and hide him in the ground: it is they
who now feel the touch of death cold in their bones.

Animals hate death. A trapped fox will gnaw
through his own leg: it is so important to live
that he forgives himself the agony,
consenting, for life's sake, to the desperate teeth
grating through bone and pulp, the gasping yelps.

That is the reason the trapper hates the fox.
You think the trapper doesn't hate the fox?
But he does, and the fox can tell how much.
It is not the fox's teeth that grind his bones,
It is the trapper's. It is the trapper, there,
Who keeps his head down, gnawing, hour after hour.

And the people the trapper works for, they are there too,
heads down beside the trap, gnawing away.
Why shouldn't they hate the fox? Their cheeks are
    smeared
with his rank blood, and on their tongues his bone
being splintered, feels uncomfortably sharp.

So once Major Eatherly hated the Japanese.

III

Hell is a furnace, so the wise men taught.
The punishment for sin is to be broiled.
A glowing coal for every sinful thought.

166

The heat of God's great furnace ate up sin,
Which whispered up in smoke or fell in ash:
So that each hour a new hour could begin.

So fire was holy, though it tortured souls,
The sinners' anguish never ceased, but still
Their sin was burnt from them by shining coals.

Hell fried the criminal but burnt the crime,
Purged where it punished, healed where it destroyed:
It was a stove that warmed the rooms of time.

No man begrudged the flames their appetite.
All were afraid of fire, yet none rebelled.
The wise men taught that hell was just and right.

'The soul desires its necessary dread:
Only among the thorns can patience weave
A bower where the mind can make its bed.'

Even the holy saints whose patient jaws
Chewed bitter rind and hands raised up the dead
Were chestnuts roasted at God's furnace doors.

The wise men passed. The clever men appeared.
They ruled that hell be called a pumpkin face.
They robbed the soul of what it justly feared.

Coal after coal the fires of hell went out.
Their heat no longer warmed the rooms of time,
Which glistened now with fluorescent doubt.

The chilly saints went striding up and down
To warm their blood with useful exercise.
They rolled like conkers through the draughty town.

Those emblematic flames sank down to rest,
But metaphysical fire can not go out:
Men ran from devils they had dispossessed,

And felt within their skulls the dancing heat
No longer stored in God's deep boiler-room.

Fire scorched their temples, frostbite chewed their
    feet.

That parasitic fire could race and climb
More swiftly than the stately flames of hell.
Its fuel gone, it licked the beams of time.

So time dried out and youngest hearts grew old
The smoky minutes cracked and broke apart.
The world was roasting but the men were cold.

Now from this pain worse pain was brought to
    birth,
More hate, more anguish, till at last they cried,
'Release this fire to gnaw the crusty earth:

Make it a flame that's obvious to sight
And let us say we kindled it ourselves,
To split the skulls of men and let in light.

Since death is camped among us, wish him joy,
Invite him to our table and our games.
We cannot judge, but we can still destroy.'

And so the curtains of the mind were drawn.
Men conjured hell a first, a second time:
And Major Eatherly took off at dawn.

IV

Suppose a sea-bird,
its wings stuck down with oil, riding the waves
in no direction, under the storm-clouds, helpless,
lifted for an instant by each moving billow
to scan the meaningless horizon, helpless,
helpless, and the storms coming, and its wings dead,
its bird-nature dead:
                Imagine this castaway,
loved, perhaps, by the Creator, and yet abandoned,
mocked by the flashing scales of the fish beneath it,

who leap, twist, dive, as free of the wide sea
as formerly the bird of the wide sky,
now helpless, starving, a prisoner of the surface,
unable to dive or rise: this is your emblem.
Take away the bird, let it be drowned
in the steep black waves of the storm, let it be
        broken
against rocks in the morning light, too faint to swim:
take away the bird, but keep the emblem.

It is the emblem of Major Eatherly,
who looked round quickly from the height of each
        wave,
but saw no land, only the rim of the sky
into which he was not free to rise, or the silver
gleam of the mocking scales of the fish diving
where he was not free to dive.

Men have clung always to emblems,
to tokens of absolution from their sins.
Once it was the scapegoat driven out, bearing
its load of guilt under the empty sky
until its shape was lost, merged in the scrub.

Now we are civilized, there is no wild heath.
Instead of the nimble scapegoat running out
to be lost under the wild and empty sky,
the load of guilt is packed into prison walls,
and men file inward through the heavy doors.

But now the image, too, is obsolete.
The Major entering prison is no scapegoat.
His penitence will not take away our guilt,
nor sort with any consoling ritual:
this is penitence for its own sake, beautiful,
uncomprehending, inconsolable, unforeseen.
He is not in prison for his penitence:
it is no outrage to our law that he wakes

with cries of pity on his parching lips.
We do not punish him for cries or nightmares.
We punish him for stealing things from stores.

O, give his pension to the storekeeper.
Tell him it is the price of all our souls.
But do not trouble to unlock the door
and bring the Major out into the sun.
Leave him: it is all one: perhaps his nightmares
grow cooler in the twilight of the prison.
Leave him; if he is sleeping, come away.
But lay a folded paper by his head,
nothing official or embossed, a page
torn from your notebook, and the words in pencil.
Say nothing of love, or thanks, or penitence:
say only 'Eatherly, we have your message.'

From

A Word Carved on a Sill

(1956)

Yet love survives, the word carved on a sill
Under antique dread of the headsman's axe
Robert Graves

Patriotic Poem

This mildewed island,
Rained on and beaten flat by bombs and water,
Seems ready now to crack like any other
Proud organism drugged with praise and torture.

History rolls
His heavy tide of insolence and wonder
Scarring her surface with as many holes
As her moth-eaten sky where fighters thunder.

Yet from the cauldron
Where her hard bones are formed by time and
        anguish
Rises the living breath of all her children;
And her deep heart and theirs, who can distinguish?

Eighth Type of Ambiguity

'Love is too young to know what conscience is,
Yet who knows not, conscience is born of love?'
It seems a meaning we could hardly miss.

Yet even such pellucid lines may prove
Unwilling to be readily construed;
Their needle travels in a double groove.

For love we find both delicate and crude;
And poets long ago began to ask
'Love rules the world, but is the world subdued?'

So understanding love is quite a task,
And Shakespeare was no more than being wise
In fitting out his statement with a mask;

For love is always seen with bleary eyes,
And conscience (meaning 'consciousness') defines
The fire that blazes in a gale of sighs.

But still for love the silly spirit pines
In searching for the logic of its dream,
In pacing endlessly those dark confines.

When love as germ invades the purple stream
It splashes round the veins and multiplies
Till objects of desire are what they seem;

Then all creation wears a chic disguise,
And consciousness becomes a clever changer
Turning a punishment into a prize.

And so to every type love is a danger.
Some think it means no more than saying Yes,
And some turn canine when they reach the
        manger.

It seems a meaning we could hardly guess.

Riddle for a Christmas Cracker

This tranquil cyclone, gentle in its rage,
This word too simple to be understood,
New-born and squalling, dignified with age:

This unforgiven crime, serene with good,
Homage of toilsome climb and steep descent,
Thirst-bringing drink, starvation-causing food;

Beyond the passion lies the deep content,
Beneath the deep content, the passion runs;
A hateful kindness, Hell-born, Heaven-sent:

Its servants in their heat as pure as nuns,
Savagely warring, blessedly at rest;
Its pulse the rising of outnumbered suns:

Its slime the vapoured dew, its worst the best,
Its sickness health, its depths the clearest sky:
What is it? Ah, you never would have guessed:

But she towards whom (though far) I softly cry
When asked, immediately would find it out,
Swiftly as white intuitive pigeons fly.

On Reading Love Poetry in the Dentist's Waiting Room

Waiting for pain I read about their joy,
How he had found her richer than the East
And wheeled his wooden horse into her Troy,

Adoring from the greatest to the least
Those qualities which lighted his quick fuse,
Yet still remained more demi-god than beast.

Such penetration how could she refuse?
He writes here that she paid him love for love.
The world was all before them where to choose

Where gently as the wing-beats of a dove
He should conduct her to the sacred cave,
And wander in her like an orange grove.

Yet in some silent sphere beyond the grave
Their pleasure and my pain shall be as one,
When all sensation, like a breaking wave,

Shall sink into the pebbles and be gone.
And then my anguish shall be their fruition:
So, thinking of the drill, I here condone

The drill they mastered with sweet intuition;
Hoping they did not breathe their vows in vain,
Nor ever found a cure for their condition,

And twine their written joy about my pain.

The Last Time

'The last time' are the hardest words to say.
The last time is the wrong time all along,
The morning when we pack and go away.

It must be true. The angel beats the gong.
The heart floods over when we thought it dry.
Sums that work out too easily are wrong.

It is not only for escape we fly.
We fly because the world is turning round
And permanence lives only in the sky.

The Red Queen's canter over shifty ground
Is the best logic, though we learn it late;
Hoping each day to balance Lost with Found;

And if, as we suspect, it is our fate
To find that what we lost was always more,
So that the ledger never works out straight

And each day finds us poorer than before;
Still it is searching makes us seem sublime,
Hoping each night to gain the happy shore,

To say there for the last time 'the last time'.

The Bad Thing

Sometimes just being alone seems the bad thing.
Solitude can swell until it blocks the sun.
It hurts so much, even fear, even worrying
Over past and future, get stifled. It has won,
You think; this is the bad thing, it is here.
Then sense comes; you go to sleep, or have
Some food, write a letter or work, get something
    clear.
Solitude shrinks; you are not all its slave.

Then you think: the bad thing inhabits yourself.
Just being alone is nothing; not pain, not balm.
Escape, into poem, into pub, wanting a friend
Is not avoiding the bad thing. The high shelf
Where you stacked the bad thing, hoping for calm,
Broke. It rolled down. It follows you to the end.

Sonnet

An animal with a heart (in the ordinary sense
of the expression) would find the going tough,
no doubt of it. Birds, to get enough
to eat, would have to peck – with no defence
against the bully Conscience – worms they were
sorry for. Dear me! And cats would shed
very hot tears for little mice, quite dead;
digested, indeed; and hedgehogs would pay dear

for beetles crunched while happily at play,
and so on, *ad lib.* Yes, if they had hearts (in
the ordinary sense) and yet still had to eat
and copulate, despite their sense of sin,
they'd be human, just like us, wouldn't they?
But our hearts beat and ache. Theirs only beat.

Cameo

Lovers like bridges arch across
dividing landscapes. Their meetings are moments
most high and innocent, their swift silences
rich. He is her city where gardens are never
frightened by storms, and stones are tranquil;
she is his tree, his lamp of joy: no more
is worth saying. Above them the sky
hangs and seems dangerous, disliking their perfection.

Index of First Lines